WOMEN AND STRESS RESEARCH

WOMEN AND STRESS RESEARCH

JAMES H. HUMPHREY

Novinka Books
New York

Library of Congress Cataloging-in-Publication Data:
Available Upon Request

ISBN: 1-59454-675-4

Published by Nova Science Publishers, Inc. ✤ New York

No one can make you feel inferior without your consent.
Eleanor Roosevelt (1884-1962)

CONTENTS

ABOUT THE AUTHOR

James H. Humphrey has authored or coauthored 60 books and edited 43 others. Several of his books have been in the area of stress. His articles and research reports have appeared in more than 20 different national and international journals and magazines. Considered a pioneer in stress education, he is the founder and editor of *Human Stress: Current Selected Research* and editor of the 16-book series on *Stress in Modern Society*. In the early 1980s he collaborated with the late Hans Selye, who is generally known as the father of stress research, on certain aspects of the subject. Dr. Humphrey has received numerous educational honors and awards. He is a Fellow in the American Institute of Stress.

FOREWORD

The manifestations and ramifications of stress have been well documented and publicized, as have the occasions and causes. Stress has increasingly become associated with increased susceptibility to various illnesses. Statistics from various surveys, organizations and government agencies indicate how serious a medical problem stress is and how costly it is from an economic and financial perspective. Economic and financial costs, however, hardly reflect all the human costs involved as a result of illness, emotional trauma and personal suffering.

The latest Centers for Disease Control reports indicate that life expectancy has increased to 79.9 years for women and 74.4 years for men. Women comprise 46% of the 137 million workers in the United States; their share in the labor force is projected to reach 48% by 2008. Work stress is the primary source of stress for American adults and female workers may be particularly affected. Women today face unprecedented pressures in accommodating the demands of home and career and the personal family stresses that often result. Biologically and behaviorally, women experience and cope with stress differently than men. Women are prone to the same stressors experienced by men and are also confronted with potentially unique physical and psychological stressors all their own. Women may also become stress "carriers," as in the abusive husband and unfair boss situation. Despite these differences, or perhaps because of them, women live longer than men, although, collectively, they reported more symptoms, illnesses, intake of drugs and doctor-hospital visits than men.

The connotation of the term "stress," in its current usage, is associated with "distress." Yet, as Hans Selye and others have shown, not all stress is bad for you. An optimal level of stress enhances human capacity and is a necessary ingredient if life is to manifest vitality.

Stress factors reportedly impinge upon homeostasis, a term describing the body's numerous mechanisms that assist in returning it to a "normal" state or baseline levels of activity. *Homeo* refers to "similar or like;" *stasis* refers to "position – ability to stay the same or static, stationary."

Sociologically, stasis refers to a condition of social life in which no changes are taking place. Change and stress are related – the more change there is per unit of time, the more stressful it is for people. The effects of rapid change are apparent in the changing roles of today's woman. Are we being victimized by stress which comes as a result of our lifestyles and the pace at which we live in this technologically sophisticated world? The proactive woman knows that, whenever possible, she needs to be discriminating in her selection of the kinds of changes she wants to bring about in her life rather than having them imposed on her by outside forces.

Pathologically, *stasis* refers to stagnation. People try to avoid extremes, both continual unpredictable changes and dull routines are stressful. Job satisfaction studies indicate that people are looking for identity, purpose and meaning in their work and few are finding these things.

Growth and development at any level involve stress and adaptation. Within the bud of any flower, tension mounts before unfoldment of its petals. Life is not a spectator sport – staying power is the heart of the matter. To grow significantly at *any* level, we must develop staying power – spiritually, mentally, emotionally as well as physically. This dynamism is reflected in our health; as Jonas Salk in "Survival of the Wisest" wrote, "by health is meant an ordered dynamic equilibrium in the process of growth, development, and evolution." We need to learn to respond trustingly to the challenges of life, "to feel existence," to exist fully in context as life presents itself and personality unfolds.

Our modern age describes the psyche as a chemical entity, the body as a machine and the manufactured world as a marvel of human brainpower and technology. The fountainhead of mind-body research is gradually changing this paradigm. As our knowledge of the mind-body connection grows, it becomes apparent that we are our own best weapons in defending ourselves against the adverse effects of stress. Stress is not to be avoided all the time –

it is to be managed – to be transmuted. Our psychic tropism needs to reorient toward the *Almighty Drive* (Hans Selye), ...the *force that through the green fuse drives...* (Dylan Thomas).

In our polytrophic lives, we all have a choice; how much of an effect will stress have upon us, how will we manage it, will we become a stress victim. In *Women and Stress: Don't be a Victim.* Dr. Humphrey addresses these various issues and helps us to transmute a perceived foe into a potential ally.

Anna Huzil, M.S.W., M.B.A.
Executive Director
The American Institute of Stress

PREFACE

Stress!!! What is it? What causes it? How does it affect women? How can they cope with it? These are some of the many questions that are dealt with in *Women and Stress: Don't be a Victim.*

To arrive at valid answers to these questions I surveyed and/or interviewed hundreds of women in various populations, using my own *Humphrey Stress Inquiry Form.* A case in point with regard to the extent of this work, was my ten percent sampling of about 40,000 nurses in the state of Maryland, Northern Virginia and the District of Columbia. The importance of and interest in this investigation was demonstrated by the 70 percent of responses received. All of my surveys of other populations showed similar results. Obviously, all of this information provided a substantial database for the book.

In recent years a voluminous amount of literature has appeared in both the scientific community and popular sources in the area of stress. After examining the literature on the subject I would estimate that about 20 percent of it pertains specifically to women. Although much of it provides valid information, some of it is misinformation and speculation.

In this book the reader should not expect to find definitive answers to the solution of problems concerned with stress. On the other hand, if the book is viewed as a *guide* rather than as a *recipe,* it is likely that more value will be derived from it.

Although numerous suggestions and recommendations are made with regard to the subject of stress, the reader should take into account that individual differences prevail in all of us. In other words, what works for one person may not work for another. It should be understood that underlying conditions causing problems of stress differ, individuals dealing with the problems differ, and procedures for dealing with the problems differ.

To summarize, the main focus of the book is to take into account many stressful conditions that are relevant to women. To this end, the intent is to familiarize the reader with some of the basic facets and ramifications of stress as well as to consider possible actions women might take in dealing with it.

Chapter 1

ABOUT WOMEN

From certain points of view, ours has been a "man's world" traditionally, although no one can say with any great confidence whether on the average, men have been happier or have had greater satisfaction in life than women.

Although various theories have been set forth, we can only speculate as to the prehistoric factors that resulted in the dominance of men. Nevertheless, their physical superiority for various activities and freedom from the periodic restrictions of weakness imposed by femininity and motherhood in women were no doubt influential considerations. Simone de Beauvoir,[1] the French philosopher and feminist, once suggested that as man rose above the animal level and began to exercise control over nature by means of tools, woman continued to be more closely bound to her animal nature and her body because of the maternal function, and the biological and economic conditions of the primitive horde must have led to male superiority. In any case, through the ages the male of the species continued to dominate the female.

By any valid measure, society has been demonstrably biased against females. No doubt it is little consolation for women to know that certain majestic and powerful things are identified by the female gender: ships at sea, even our country ("stand beside *her* and guide *her*"), and of course, "Mother Nature."

Although there are some who will never want to absolve women from the "sin" of Eve for "Adam's folly," many successful efforts to diminish sex discrimination have been made over the years. Indeed, a phenomenon of modern times is the vast changes in female behavior and the assertiveness of the female personality. Despite the difficulties encountered in breaking down some of the barriers, "You've come a long way baby" when it is considered that in the 16th century the Council at Macon decided by only one vote that women did have a soul.[2]

It is the primary function of this initial chapter to examine some of the changes in the status of women in modern times with particular reference to the "infiltration" of women into areas previously dominated almost entirely by men.

EDUCATION OF WOMEN

Back in the days when women were supposed to be "barefoot and pregnant," it was believed that there was little need for them to be educated. This was pretty much typical of the thinking that women were somehow inferior to men.

In the early American Common Schools (elementary schools) there were scattered examples of *coeducation* in the late 17th century. But there was no great trend until the expansion of public education between 1830 and 1845 in the developing Western United States. The distance between schools in that region and the small number of pupils caused elementary schools to admit girls. The movement spread naturally to the secondary schools during the reorganization of public education after the Civil War.[3]

The right to be freely admitted to a college or university of one's choice came slowly to females. Scholarships and grants have traditionally gone more readily to men. At one time the question arose as to what educational degree should be conferred upon women. The awarding of a bachelor's or master's degree did not seem appropriate, so for a time such degrees as "Laureate of Science," "Maid of Philosophy," or "Mistress of Polite Literature" were conferred.[4]

In modern times, according to the United States department of Education, the percentage of female high school graduates enrolling in college is now larger than males. In 1970, five million college students were male and three and one-half were female. In contrast, in 1989 7.3 million were female and 6.5 million were male.

More recently, however, at colleges and universities throughout the United States, the proportion of bachelor's degrees awarded to women in 2002 was estimated at 57 percent. Men had made up the majority of the nation's college graduates since at least 1870, when the first national survey of bachelor's degrees awarded by colleges and universities found 7,993 male graduates and 1,378 female. Except for a brief period during World War II, that remained the case until female college enrollment began outnumbering men in the late 1970s. By the early 1980s, women began outnumbering men among four-year college graduates. Since then, the number of female bachelor's degree recipients has risen to 698,000 in 2002 according to United States Department of Education estimates. The number of male college graduates has increased more slowly, to 529,000.[5]

Some researchers are concerned that the trend could herald a shift in the nation's social dynamic, with educated women unable to find mates of equal educational background. A very profound calculation is that business groups are beginning to worry about a possible dwindling share of men to fill top corporate jobs.

Talk about a prognostication – almost 2,500 years ago Socrates, the renowned Greek philosopher is reputed to have said, "Once made equal to man, woman becomes his 'superior.'" And it looks more and more like it could come to pass. Of course, the downside to all of the above is that it could predispose women to more stressful conditions.

FEMINISM

Feminism is organized activity on behalf of women's rights and interests. It is a movement for the political, social, and educational equality of women and men. It had its roots in the humanism of the 18th century and in the Industrial Revolution, both of which contributed to the emergence of society from a feudal aristocracy to an industrial democracy.

Because women were regarded as inferior to men, they could not in their own names possess property, engage in business or control the disposal of their children or even of their own persons.

The feminist movement in this country actually got its start in 1848 when Elizabeth Cady Stanton and others, at a women's convention at Seneca Falls, New York issued a declaration of independence for women. They demanded full legal equality, full educational and commercial opportunity, equal compensation and the right to collect wages and the right to vote. Elizabeth Cady Stanton was one of the founding mothers of the 19th century women's rights movement and an organizer of the first convention on women's rights in 1848. She is credited with the following statement:[6]

"But standing alone we learned our power; we repudiated man's counsels forevermore and solemnly vowed that there should never be another season of silence until we had the same rights everywhere on this earth, as man."

The movement spread rapidly and little by little women's demands for higher education, entrance into all trades and professions, married women's property and other rights, and the right to vote, were conceded.

In the United States after woman's suffrage was won in 1920, women were divided on the question of equal standing with men (advocated by the National Woman's Party) versus some protective legislation. Various forms of protective legislation had been enacted in the 19th century such as limiting the number of hours women could work per week and excluding women from certain high-risk occupations.

In 1946 the United Nations Commission on the Status of Women was established to secure equal political rights, economic rights, and educational opportunities for women throughout the world. In the 1960s feminism, or the Women's Liberation movement as it became known, experienced a rebirth especially in the United States. The National Organization for Women (NOW) was formed in 1966. This organization has developed into a very powerful political force and has attracted hundreds of thousands of supporters in various marches in behalf of women.

Congress passed the Equal Rights Amendment in 1972. This Amendment, requiring ratification by 38 states, would ban sex discrimination at the national level. The political aspects of the Women's movement have been phenomenal as we shall see in the following discussion.

WOMEN IN POLITICS

Any discussion of women in politics needs to begin with woman suffrage, because the first entry into politics comes with the right to vote. As mentioned previously, women's voting rights were first seriously proposed in the United States in a general declaration of the rights of women by Elizabeth Cady Stanton and others. The early leaders of the movement - Susan B. Anthony, Elizabeth Cady Stanton and others - were usually advocates of temperance and the abolition of slavery. When, however, after the end of the Civil War, the 15th Amendment of 1870 gave the franchise to newly emancipated Black men, but not to the women who had helped to win if for them, the suffragists continued their efforts to struggle for the vote.

The National Woman Suffrage Association, led by Susan B. Anthony, Elizabeth Cady Stanton and others, was formed in 1869 to agitate for an amendment to the Federal Constitution. Another organization, The American Woman Suffrage Association led by Lucy Stone was organized the same year to work through the state legislatures. These differing approaches – whether to seek a Federal amendment or to work for state amendments – kept the women suffrage movement divided until 1890. At this time the two organizations were united as the National American Woman Suffrage Association. Several of the states and territories (with Wyoming first in 1869) granted suffrage to the women within their borders. When in 1913 there were 12 of these, the National Woman's party resolved to use the voting power of the enfranchised women to force a suffrage resolution through Congress and secure ratification from the state legislatures. And finally, in 1920, the 19th Amendment to the Constitution granted nation-wide suffrage to women.

When World War I broke out the suffragists ceased all militant activity and devoted their powerful organization to the service of the government. After the war a limited suffrage was granted. In 1928 voting rights for men and women were equalized.

Although women have held the office of Mayor in some large cities and Governor in some large states, this country has lagged behind in electing women as heads of state. Early leaders in this regard were Israel (Golda Meir), India (Indira Gandhi), and Great Britain (Margaret Thatcher). The highest nomination any woman has received in this country was that of Vice President by Geraldine A. Ferraro on the Democratic ticket in 1984.

There have been rare instances when women ran for the Presidency – Shirley Chisholm in 1972 and Patricia Schroeder in 1988. Known as "Fighting Shirley Chisholm," she was the first African American woman to run for President. She started out as a teacher, was elected as a Congresswoman for New York, and she continued to work to strengthen education and to help the poor. She once expressed her philosophy as follows:[7]

"U.S. Politics is a beautiful fraud that has been imposed on the people for years, whose practitioners exchange gelded promises for the most valuable thing their victims own, their votes."

Patricia Schroeder, a Representative from Colorado was characterized as follows, by Judy Mann, former feature writer for *The Washington Post,* in her book, *Mann for All Seasons:*[8]

"She was able to make her points trenchantly when she accused the American military establishment of having a serious case of 'missile envy.'"

Fifteen years later on February 19, 2003, Carol Moseley-Braun, the only African American woman elected to the United States Senate announced her candidacy for President in 2004 with the comment: "It's time to take the Men Only sign off the White House door."[9]

A question to ponder is: Why is it that many women do not run for President? A report on a survey[10] by the National Women's Political Caucus provided part of the answer. For the first time, when a male and female candidate for office were matched head to head, the public chose the woman; that is, Ms. X beat Mr. X. However, when the same people were asked if they thought the woman would win, they answered "no." The voters appear to have less confidence that a woman candidate can win - and perhaps so do women candidates themselves. A modern woman aspiring to a high political office might well heed the words of Eleanor Roosevelt: *No one can make you feel inferior without your consent.*

Although *gynecocracy* (political supremacy of women) may be some time down the road, it is clearly evident that women are fast becoming a strong political force. Let us examine the premise.

To begin with, women comprise a majority of the electorate; thus, they start with superiority in numbers. In a survey[11] conducted for the National Association of Female Executives more than half of the women polled said Senate hearings on the confirmation of Clarence Thomas to the Supreme Court made them consider women's issues in the Presidential election more than they would otherwise have done. In fact, this action incensed many women to the extent that they banded together to defeat those Senators who supported the Thomas confirmation.

On the basis of my own studies, my estimate would be that by the year 2010 there will be as many as 30 female Senators, and more than 100 members of the House of Representatives. This could be too generous a prediction but at the rate women are now exerting their political power, it could well be within the realm of possibility.

WOMEN IN THE MEDIA

As in many other forms of endeavor, women appear to have been dealt with the worst of it as far as the media are concerned. The following comment by the previously-mentioned Judy Mann, lucidly points up the discrepancy:

"A group of White men gather around a table every day at major media outlets to decide what you will hear on the news or what you will read in the following day's paper. They decide what is news."

If this is the case, there is no question that we could be ill-informed if more than one half of the population is not able to decide what is news.

A serious controversial matter regarding sports reporting is that which is concerned with female access to male locker rooms. The classic case of Lisa Olson, former sportswriter for the Boston Herald, reached an out-of-court settlement in her sexual harassment case in which she alleged that New England Patriots players taunted her before a locker room interview. The exact amount of the settlement was not published, but it was said to be substantial. Ms. Olson was quoted as saying, "Hopefully, some good will come of this. I hope in 10 years' time, no person man or woman, will have to go through this just for doing his or her job."[12]

Since the early 1990s things have grown progressively for women in the media in both *print* and *broadcast* journalism. More and more newspaper reporters and talk show participants are of the female gender.

A possible precursor to this movement was the election of Helen Thomas, who at the time was the dean of White House correspondents, as the first women president of the National Press Club of Washington in 1992. This organization had previously restricted its membership to men.

WOMEN IN THE LAW PROFESSION

The under representation of women in high status traditional male professions can likely be attributed to sex-role socialization and discrimination. However, the gender gap is decreasing at a phenomenal rate. For example, Law is a formerly male dominated profession that has been "invaded" by women in the past few years. Since the early 1970s, the number of women who practice law in the United States increased from 12,000 to 116,000. It is reasonable to expect that by 2010 well over one-half of all American lawyers will be women. A question to ponder is: Will the high proportion of women to be found in the legal profession result in their full acceptance at the highest levels of the profession, or will they be kept at a secondary level, as has occurred in other professions?

It is interesting to note that a study conducted by the Washington State Bar Association[13] found that there is decreased satisfaction among lawyers with the job. The survey found that 55 percent of all lawyers in private practice reported not having enough time for themselves and 45 percent said they did not have enough time for their families. Many of those demands were heightened for *women lawyers* who often bear more of the burden for child care and, unlike many of their men counterparts, virtually never have a stay-at-home spouse to ease demands at home.

Another aspect of the law, *law enforcement,* is an area where women have made some strides over the years. Elizabeth Watson made history in 1990 when she was appointed the first female police chief in a major American city – Houston, Texas (because of a change in administration, she stepped down to the assistant chief in March 1992).

In a provocative article in *Time* on February 17, 1992, Jeanne McDowell[14] asserted that while women constitute only nine percent of the nation's police officers, they are bringing a distinctly different and valuable set of skills to the streets and the station house that may change the way the police are perceived in the community. And, further, as the job description expands beyond crime fighting to community service, the growing presence of women may help burnish a tarnished image of police officers, improve community relations and foster a more flexible and less violent approach to keeping the peace.

The road ahead for women in policing may be a difficult one because affirmative action programs in the public sector are necessarily affected by political and economic trends. The conservative political environment, coupled with the advent of serious fiscal constraints facing many cities, raises questions about whether it is reasonable to expect progress in the employment of women in non-traditional roles in municipal governments. This question was investigated a while back by analyzing data gathered from reported surveys of more than 280 municipal police departments in large United States cities.[15] Findings indicated that women can expect great difficulty and long delays in improving their representation in municipal policing. Municipal budget reductions, increasing numbers of court cases that challenge the legality of affirmative hiring, promotion and firing policies, and a conservative political environment, emphasizing individual rights over social equity, are seen as causes of this delay.

WOMEN IN THE MEDICAL PROFESSION

The number of female physicians is increasing by leaps and bounds. In 1970, eight percent of medical degrees were awarded to women compared to 33 percent going to women in 1989. This rose to more than 40 percent in

2002. (It should be mentioned that all women who receive medical degrees do not go into medical practice because in many instances they take other jobs that require a medical background). In medicine, there are more than 50 specialties in addition to general practice. Although the barriers to specialization such as orthopedics are no longer great, women still tend to choose pediatrics, obstetrics-gynecology, psychiatry, anesthesiology, internal medicine, and family medicine.

Although the 104,000 women practicing medicine in 1992 accounted for only 17 percent of the nation's doctors, by 2010 the American Medical Association projects that 30 percent of all doctors will be women. The impact is likely to be most dramatic in the previously-mentioned medical fields favored by women. In pediatrics and child psychiatry, for example, women account for one-half of all residents (new medical school graduates training in a specialty) according to the Association of American Medical Colleges.

However, such good news is tempered by persistent complaints of subtle sexism toward women entering the profession. Women-doctors and students complain that few women are in high positions at medical schools, and they are promoted more slowly, that women reported having been the object of sexual advances, and nearly one-third feel they have been denied opportunities in their training because they were women.

Although medicine is potentially one of the most prestigious and higher-paying health professions, it can also be one of the most stressful. Being surrounded by sickness and death can lead to many stress-related problems for physicians. Some women take the stressors of medicine personally as shown in these alarming findings: Female medical students and physicians have higher rates than their male counterparts of drug addiction, alcoholism, and depression and the rate of suicide is four to one over that of the general female population.

In summary, there is do doubt about it, women have been and will continue more and more to be important leaders in our society. Take the case of sheer numbers alone. At about age 30 the population is about equally divided between males and females. However, by the nonagenarian stage women outnumber men by more than three to one. Moreover, my own studies reveal that women currently own about 60 percent of the automobiles in this country; and this could increase to 75 percent by 2015. Would we dare speculate that they will own all of the cars by 2040?

Finally, women have not always been given due credit for being inventive, and it is not well known that nuclear fission, pink champagne, solar heating, drip coffee, and the ice cream cone were all invented by women.

(*Note*: Later chapters will go into detail on stress in professions dominated by women)

Chapter 2

ABOUT STRESS

There is an unbelievable amount of confusion surrounding the meaning of stress and related terms. For this reason it appears important to attempt to arrive at some operational definitions and descriptions of some of these terms. If this can be accomplished, it will make for much easier communication in dealing with stress.

An intelligent discussion of any subject should perhaps begin with some sort of understanding about the terminology concerning the given subject. There are several important reasons why a book on stress, in particular, should begin by establishing such a general frame of reference. For one thing, a review of several hundred pieces of literature concerned with stress revealed that the terminology connected with it is voluminous, sometimes contradictory and, to say the least, rather confusing. Many times, terms with different meanings are likely to be used interchangeably; conversely the same term may be used under various circumstances to denote several different meanings. That this results in confusion for the reader is obvious, because such usage of terminology is likely to generate a situation of multiple meanings in the general area of stress. In this regard, my interviews and surveys with individuals at all age levels revealed a wide variety of understandings with reference to the meaning of stress.

It should be understood that the purpose is not to develop a set of standardized stress-related terms. This would be well-nigh impossible. The purpose is for communication only, and limited to the aims of this particular book. In other words, if a term is used in this book you will know what is meant by it. The idea is to try to develop working descriptions of terms for the purpose of communicating with you, the reader. In no sense is it intended to impose a terminology upon you. If you prefer other terms you should feel free to use them in your communication with others.

For the discussion of terminology that follows, there will be an effort to resort in some instances to terms used by various authorities in the field, and in others, insofar as they may be available, to use pure technical definitions. It should be understood that many of the terms have some sort of general meaning. An attempt will be made in some cases to start with this general meaning and give it specific meaning for the subject at hand.

STRESS

There is no solid agreement regarding the derivation of the term stress. For example, it is possible that the term is derived from the Latin word *stringere,* which means to "bind tightly." Or it could have derived from the French word *destress,* anglicized to *distress.* The prefix *dis* could eventually have been eliminated because of slurring, as in the case of the word *because* sometimes becoming *'cause.*

A common generalized literal description of stress is "a constraining force or influence." When applied to the human organism, this could be interpreted to mean the extent to which the body can withstand a given force or influence. In this regard one of the most often quoted descriptions of stress is that of the famous pioneer in the field, the late Hans Selye who described it as the nonspecific response of the body to any demand made upon it.[1] This means that stress involves a mobilization of the body's resources in response to a stimulus (stressor). These responses can include various physical and chemical changes in the organism. This description of stress could be extended by saying that it involves demands that tax or exceed the resources of the human organism. (Selye's concept of stress will be explained in detail later in the chapter.) This means that stress not only involves these bodily responses but also involves wear and tear on the organism brought about by these responses.

In essence, stress can be considered as being any factor, acting internally or externally, that makes it difficult to adapt and indicates increased effort on the part of the individual to maintain a state of equilibrium between herself and the external environment. It is emphasized that stress is a *state* that one is in, and this should not be confused with any agent that produces such a state. Such agents are referred to as stressors.

Understanding the meaning of stress can be made more difficult because certain stress-related terms can cause confusion. Therefore, it seems appropriate at this point to review the meaning of such terms as tension, emotion, anxiety, burnout and depression.

TENSION

The term tension is very frequently used in relation to stress and thus, attention should be given to the meaning of this term. It is interesting to examine the entries used for these terms in the *Education Index*. This bibliographical index of periodical educational literature records entries on the terms stress and tension as follows:

- *Stress* (physiology);
- *Stress* (psychology) see Tension (psychology);
- *Tension* (physiology) see *Tension* (physiology);
- Tension (psychology).

This indicates that there are physiological and psychological aspects of both stress and tension. However, articles in the periodical literature listed as "stress" articles seem to imply that stress is more physiologically oriented and that tension is more psychologically oriented. Thus, psychological stress and psychological tension could be interpreted to mean the same thing. The breakdown in this position is seen where there is another entry for tension concerned with *muscular* tension. The latter, of course must be considered to have a physiological orientation. In the final analysis, the validity of these entries will depend upon the point of view of each individual. As we shall see later, the validity of this particular cataloging of these terms may possibly be at odds with a more specific meaning of the term.

Tensions can be viewed in two frames of reference; first, as *physiologic* or *unlearned* tensions, and second, as *psychologic* or *learned* tensions. An example of the first, physiologic or unlearned tensions, would be "tensing" at bright lights or intense sounds. Psychologic or learned tensions are responses to stimuli that ordinarily do not involve muscular contractions, but that at some time earlier in a person's experience were associated with a situation in which tension was a part of the normal response. In view of the fact that the brain connects any events that stimulate it simultaneously, it would appear that, depending upon the unlimited kinds of personal experiences one might have, he or she may show tension to any and all kinds of stimuli. An example of psychologic or learned tension would be an inability to relax when riding in a car after experiencing or imagining too many automobile accidents.

In a sense, it may be inferred that physiologic or unlearned tensions are current and spontaneous, while psychologic or learned tensions may be latent as a result of a previous experience and may emerge at a later time.

Although there may be a hairline distinction between stress and tension in the minds of some people, perhaps an essential difference between stress and tension is that the former is a physical and/or mental state concerned with wear and tear on the organism, while the latter is either a spontaneous or latent condition which brings about this wear and tear.

EMOTION

Since the terms stress and emotion are used interchangeably in some literature, consideration should be given to the meaning of the latter term. Emotion could be viewed as the response an individual makes when confronted with a situation for which she is unprepared or which is interpreted as a possible source of gain or loss. For example, if one is confronted with a situation for which she may not have a satisfactory response, the emotional pattern of fear could result. Or, if a person is in a position where desires are frustrated, the emotional pattern of anger may occur. Emotion, then, is not the state of stress itself but rather it is a stressor that can stimulate stress. (The subject of emotions will be discussed in detail in Chapter 5.)

ANXIETY

Another term used to mean the same thing as stress is anxiety. In fact, some of the literature uses the expression "anxiety *or* stress" implying that they are one and the same thing. This can lead to the chicken and egg controversy. That is, is stress the cause of anxiety or is anxiety the cause of stress? Or, is it a reciprocal situation?

A basic literal meaning of anxiety is "uneasiness of the mind," but this simple generalization may be more complex than one might think. C. Eugene Walker, a notable clinical psychologist and a contributor to my *Human Stress Series,* once pointed out the fact that psychologists who deal with this area in detail have difficulty in defining the term. He gives as his own description of it "the reaction to a situation where we believe our well-being is endangered or threatened in some way."[2] David Viscott, another long-time authoritative source, considers anxiety as the "fear of hurt or loss." He contends that this leads to anger, with anger leading to guilt, and guilt, if unrelieved, leading to depression.[3]

BURNOUT

Some persons become unable to cope with the physical and emotional trauma generated by the demands on their energy, emotions, and time. Research conducted on people-oriented occupations indicates that some are characterized by several built-in sources of frustration, that eventually lead dedicated workers to become ineffective and apathetic; that is, burned out. Persons who experience burnout may begin to perceive their job as impossible. They may begin to question their ability. Feeling helpless and out of control, persons nearing burnout may tire easily and may experience headaches and/or digestive problems. In some cases they will view their tasks and their profession to be increasingly-meaningless, trivial or irrelevant.

With regard to burnout, a study of college athletes by William C. Thomas is of interest.[4] He hypothesized that the personality trait known as *hardiness* could mediate the effects of stress that lead to burnout. And further, hardiness, according to him, is one characteristic that could differentiate between individuals who are able to effectively manage environmental and internal demands and those who burnout.

The purpose of the study was to examine a theoretical model in which hardiness was posited to act as a stress buffer in the stress-burnout relationship. Participants were 181 National Collegiate Athletic Association Division I athletes who completed questionnaires containing stress, hardiness, and burnout instruments.

The study revealed that hardiness did appear to act as a buffer against the effect of stress. Given the positive consequences of having a hardier personality, it was concluded that athletes could benefit from purposefully structured experiences to enhance hardiness and improve their ability to cope with the many situational demands placed on them.

DEPRESSION

The term depression, as used here, is thought of as a painful emotional reaction characterized by intense feelings of loss, sadness, worthlessness, failure, or rejection not warranted by an objective view of events. Depression is often a disproportionately intense reaction to difficult life situations. It may be accompanied by such physiological symptoms as tension, slowing of mental arid motor activity, fatigue, lack of appetite and insomnia; that is, some of the same symptoms accompanying undesirable stress.

Depression can be a manifestation of many different psychomotor and physical disorders and a normal response to certain types of stress. Unless the cause of it can be clearly identified, depression usually represents a description rather than a diagnosis.

An estimated 15 percent of the population develops an episode of depression requiring medical intervention at some point in life, and stress is not the only cause.[5] Some people are born with a biological predisposition to get depressed, tending toward a brain chemical imbalance that favors a depressed mental state. In some situations the depression appears to come from nowhere, even in the best of circumstances. Perhaps more frequently than not, the depression stems from a combination of stressful life events and internal biological factors.

So much for terminology. Although the above brief discussion of certain terms does not exhaust the vocabulary used in relation to stress, it is hoped, that it will serve to help the reader distinguish the use of terms basic to an understanding of the general area of stress. Other terminology will be described as needed when dealing with certain specific topics in subsequent discussions.

In recent years the study of stress (stressology) has become widespread. Physicians, psychiatrists, psychologists, sociologists, nurses, teachers, in fact, individuals in almost all professional fields are becoming more and more concerned with the subject. In addition, leaders in business and industry have seen such an important need for stress management that many of these organizations are beginning to provide services to help employees cope with stress.

The area of stress is complicated and complex and there is a need for a better understanding of it by all segments of the population. It is the purpose of the rest of this chapter to provide basic information that may assist in improving the knowledge of the reader about this phenomenon.

THEORIES OF STRESS

It should perhaps be mentioned at this point that it is not the intent to get into a highly technical discourse on the complex aspects of stress. However, there are certain basic understandings that need to be taken into account, and this requires the use of certain technical terms. For this reason, it appears appropriate to provide an "on-the-spot" glossary of terms used in the discussion that will follow.

ACTH: (AdrenoCorticoTropic Hormone) secreted by the pituitary gland. It influences the function of the adrenals and other glands in the body.

Adrenals: Two glands in the upper posterior part of the abdomen that produce and secrete hormones. They have two parts, the outer layer, called the *cortex* and the inner layer called the *medulla*.

Corticoids: Hormones produced by the adrenal cortex, an example of which is *cortisone*.

Endocrine: Glands that secrete their hormones into the blood stream.

Hormone: A chemical that is produced by a gland, secreted into the blood stream, and influences the function of cells or organs.

Hypothalamus: The primary activator of the autonomic nervous system; it plays a central role in translating neurological stimuli into endocrine processes during stress reactions.

Pituitary: An endocrine gland located at the base of the brain that is about the size of a pea. It secretes important hormones, one of which is the ACTH hormone.

Thymus: A ductless gland that is considered a part of the endocrine gland system, and is located behind the upper part of the breast bone.

Although there are various theories of stress, one of the better known and widely accepted ones in that of the previously-mentioned Hans Selye. Selye's description of stress has already been given as the "nonspecific response of the body to any demand made upon it." The physiological processes and the reactions involved in Selye's stress model are known as the *General Adaptation Syndrome* and consist of three stages of *alarm reaction, resistance stage,* and the *exhaustion stage.*

In the first stage (alarm reaction), the body reacts to the stressor and causes the hypothalamus to produce a biochemical "messenger," which in turn causes the pituitary gland to secrete ACTH into the blood. This hormone then causes the adrenal gland to discharge adrenaline and other corticoids. This causes shrinkage of the thymus with an influence on heart rate, blood pressure, and the like. It is during the alarm stage that the resistance of the body is reduced.

In the second stage, *resistance* develops if the stressor is not too pronounced. Body adaptation develops to fight back the stress or possibly avoid it, and the body begins to repair damage, if any is present.

The third stage of *exhaustion* occurs if there is long-continued exposure to the same stressor. The ability of adaptation is eventually exhausted and the signs of the first stage (alarm reaction) reappear. Selye contended that our adaptation resources are limited, and, when they become irreversible, the result is death. Our objective, of course, should be to retain our resistance and capacity for adaptation, and this is a part of what this book is about.

Selye's stress model, which places emphasis upon "nonspecific" responses, has been widely accepted. However, the nonspecific nature of stress has been questioned by some. This means that psychological stressors activate other endocrine systems in addition to those activated by physiological stressors such as cold, electric shock, and the like.

As in the case of all research, the search for truth will continue, and more and more precise and sophisticated procedures will emerge in the scientific study of stress. Current theories will be more critically appraised and evaluated, and other theories will continue to be advanced. In the meantime, there is abundant evidence to support the notion that stress in modern society is a most serious threat to the well-being of man, if not controlled, and of course that the most important factor in such control is man himself.

REACTIONS TO STRESS

There are various ways in which reactions to stress may be classified and, in any kind of classification, there will be some degree of unavoidable overlapping. In the discussion here, I arbitrarily suggest two broad classifications as being *physiological* and *behavioral*.

Physiological Reactions

Although all individuals do not always react in the same way physiologically as far as stress is concerned, the following generalized list suggests some of the more or less standard reactions.

1. Rapid beating of the heart, which has sometimes been described as "pounding of the heart." We have all experienced this reaction at one time or another as a result of great excitement, or as a result of being afraid.
2. Perspiration, which is mostly of the palms of the hands, although there may be profuse sweating in some individuals at various other parts of the body.
3. Blood pressure rises, which may be referred to as a hidden reaction because the individual is not likely to be aware of it.

4. The pupils of the eyes may dilate and, again, the individual will not necessarily be aware of it.
5. The stomach seems to "knot up," and we tend to refer to this as "feeling a lump in the pit of the stomach." This of course can have a negative influence on digestion.
6. Sometimes individuals experience difficulty in swallowing, which is often referred to as a "lump in the throat."
7. There may be a "tight" feeling in the chest and when the stressful condition is relieved one may refer to it as "getting a load off my chest."

What these various bodily reactions mean is that the organism is gearing up for a response to a stressor. This phenomenon is called the *fight or flight* response and was first described as an *emergency* reaction by Walter B. Cannon,[6] the famous Harvard University Professor of Physiology. The fight or flight response prepares us for action in the same way that it did for prehistoric man when he was confronted with an enemy. His responses were decided on the basis of the particular situation, such as fighting an opponent for food or fleeing from an animal that provided him with an overmatched situation. In modern times, with all of the potentially stressful conditions that provoke a fight or flight response, modern man uses these same physiological responses to face up to these kinds of situations, However, today we generally do not need to fight physically (although we might feel like it sometimes), or run from wild animals, but our bodies still react with the same fight or flight response. Physiologists point out that we still need this means of self-preservation occasionally, but not in response to the emotional traumas and anxieties of modern living.

Behavioral Reactions

In discussing behavioral reactions, it should be mentioned again that various degrees of unavoidable overlapping may occur between these reactions and physiological reactions. Although behavioral reactions are, for the most part physically oriented, they are likely to involve more overt manifestations than are provoked by the physiological reactions. For the purposes of this discussion, I will consider *behavior* to mean anything that the organism does as a result of some sort of stimulation.

An individual under stress will function with a behavior that is different from ordinary behavior. These are subclassified as: (1) *counter* behavior (sometimes referred to as defensive behavior), (2) *dysfunctional* behavior, and (3) *overt* behavior (sometimes referred to as expressive behavior).

In counter behavior, a person will sometimes take action that is intended to counteract the stressful condition. An example is when an individual takes a defensive position; that is, a person practicing an "on-the-spot" relaxation technique, but at the same time, being unaware of it. She may take a deep breath and silently "count to ten" before taking action, if any.

Dysfunctional behavior means that a person will react in a manner that demonstrates impaired or abnormal functioning, which results in a lower level of skill performance than she is ordinarily capable of accomplishing. There may be changes in the normal speech patterns, and there may be a temporary impairment of the systems of perception, as well as temporary loss of memory. Many of us have-experienced this at one time or another due to a stress-inducing situation, with a "mental block" causing some degree of frustration while we attempt to get back to the original train of thought.

Overt behavior involves such reactions as distorted facial expressions; that is, tics and twitches and biting the lip. There appears to be a need for the person to move about, and thus, pacing around the room is characteristic of this condition. Incidentally, there is a point of view that suggests that overt behavior in the form of activity is preferable for most individuals in most stressful situations, and can be highly effective in reducing threat and distress.

CLASSIFICATIONS OF STRESS

The difficulty encountered in attempting to devise a foolproof classification system for the various kinds of stress should be obvious. The reason for this, of course, lies in the fact that it is practically impossible to fit a given type of stress into one exclusive category because of the possibility of overlapping. As in the case of attempting to classify reactions to stress in the immediately preceding discussion we are confronted with the same problem, in trying to classify various kinds of stress. However, an attempt will be made to do so, and, as mentioned before, any such classification on the part of the author is arbitrary. Others may wish to use different classifications than those used here, and, in the absence of anything resembling standardization, it is their prerogative to do so. With this idea in mind, some general classification of stress that will be dealt with in the following discussion are (1) desirable and undesirable stress, (2) physical stress, (3) psychological stress, and (4) social stress. It should be understood that this does not exhaust the possibilities of various kinds of stress classifications. That is, this particular listing is not necessarily theoretically complete, but for purposes here it should suffice.

Desirable and Undesirable Stress

The classic comment once made by Selye that "stress is the spice of life" sums up the idea that stress can be desirable as well as devastating. He went on to say that the only way one could avoid stress would be to never do anything and that certain kinds of activities have a beneficial influence in keeping the stress mechanism in good shape. Certainly the human organism needs to be taxed in order to function well, and it is a well-known physiological fact that muscles will soon atrophy if not subjected to sufficient use.

At one time or another most of us have experienced "butterflies in the stomach" when faced with a particularly challenging situation. Thus, it is important that we understand that stress is a perfectly normal human state and that the organism is under various degrees of stress in those conditions that are related to happiness as well as those concerned with sadness.

In the literature, undesirable stress may be referred to as *distress*. It is interesting to note that Selye referred to the pleasant or healthy kind of stress as *eustress* and to the unpleasant or unhealthy kind as *distress*.

Some of the desirable features of stress have been mentioned, but like any factor involving the human organism, most anything in excess is not good for it. Of course, this holds true for an abnormal amount of stress as well. When stress becomes prolonged and unrelenting, and thus chronic, it can result in serious trouble. In the final analysis, the recommendation is not necessarily to avoid stress, but to keep it from becoming a chronic condition.

Although both *good* stress and *bad* stress reactions place specific demands for resources on the body, does this mean that good stress is *safe* and bad stress *dangerous?* Two prominent psychologists, Israel Posner and Lewis Leitner[7] feel that two psychological variables, *predictability* and *controllability* play an important role. Let us examine this premise.

It can be reasoned that *predictable* pain and discomfort is less stressful because under this condition a person could be capable of learning when it is safe to "lower her guard" and relax. Since periods of impending pain are clearly signaled, the person can safely relax at the times when the warning is absent. These periods of psychological safety seem to insulate the individual from harmful effects of stress. Obviously, persons receiving unsignaled pain have no way of knowing when it is safe to relax and thus are more likely to develop serious health problems as a result of chronic psychological stress.

The second psychological variable, *controllability* of environmental stressors, which is closely related to coping behavior, also plays a major role in determining stress effects. The ability to control painful events may insulate individuals from experiencing damaging stress effects. However, such coping behavior is beneficial only if a person is given a feedback signal that informs her that the coping response was successful in avoiding an impending stressor. Without the feedback of success, active coping behavior, as such, may increase stress effects since it calls upon the energy reserves of the body and leaves it in a state of chronic stress.

The research on predictability and controllability of stressful events may help to answer *why* people who seek out stressful and challenging types of jobs do not appear to develop stress illnesses from this form of stress. In contrast, when essentially similar body reactivity is produced by *bad* stress, then stress-related illnesses can be the result. Perhaps *good* stress does not produce illness because typically the events associated with it are planned in advance (they are predictable) or otherwise scheduled to integrate (they are controlled) into the individual's life. However, even activities that are generally considered to be pleasant and exciting (good stress) can produce illness if the individual is not forewarned or has little control over the events. And unpleasant events (bad stress) may result in stress-related illness because they generally come without warning and cannot be controlled.

In closing this section of the chapter, it should be mentioned that some persons have taken the middle ground on this subject by saying that stress is neither good nor bad, indicating that the effect of stress is not determined by the stress itself but how it is viewed and handled. That is, we either handle stress properly or we allow it to influence us negatively and thus, become victims of undesirable stress.

Physical Stress

In discussing physical stress it is important to differentiate between the two terms *physical* and *physiological*. The former should be considered a broad term and can be described as "pertaining or relating to the body." On the other hand, physiological is concerned with what the organs do in relation to each other. Thus, physical stress could be concerned with unusual and excessive physical exertion, as well as certain physiological conditions brought about by some kind of stress.

Although there are many kinds of physical stress, they can perhaps be separated into two general types, to which the organism may react in different ways. One type may be referred to as *emergency* stress and the other *continuing* stress. In emergency stress, the previously described physiological phenomenon takes place. When an emergency arises such as bodily injury, hormones are discharged into the blood stream. This involves an increase in heart rate, rise in blood pressure, and dilation of the blood vessels in the muscles to prepare themselves for immediate use of the energy that is generated.

In continuing stress, the body's reaction is somewhat more complex. The physiological involvement is the same, but more and more hormones continue to be produced, the purpose of which is to increase body resistance. In cases where the stress is excessive, such as an extensive third degree burn, a third phase in the form of exhaustion of the adrenal glands can develop, sometimes culminating in fatality.

It was mentioned that physical stress can also be thought of as unusual and excessive physical exertion. This can be depicted in a general way by performing an experiment involving some mild physical exertion. First, try to find your resting pulse. This can be done by placing your right wrist, palm facing you, in your left hand. Now, bring the index and middle fingers of your left hand around the wrist and press lightly until you feel the beat of your pulse. Next, time this beat for ten seconds and then multiply this by six. This will give you your resting pulse rate per minute. For example, if you counted 12 beats in ten seconds, your resting pulse will be 72 beats per minute. The next step is to engage in some physical activity. Stand and balance yourself on one foot. Hop up and down on this foot for a period of about 15 seconds, or less if it is too strenuous. Then take your pulse rate again in the same manner as suggested above. You will find that, as a result of this activity, your pulse rate will be elevated above the resting pulse. Even with this small amount of physical exertion, the body was adjusting to cope with it, as evidenced by the rise in pulse rate. This was discernible to you; however, other things, such as a slight rise in blood pressure were likely involved and you were not aware of them.

Psychological Stress

The essential difference between physical stress and psychological stress is that the former involves a real situation, while psychological stress is more concerned with foreseeing or imagining an emergency situation. As an example, a vicarious experience of danger may be of sufficient intensity to cause muscle tension and elevate the heart rate. A specific example of psychological stress is seen in what is commonly called "stage fright." Incidentally, it is interesting to note that this type of psychological stress may start when one is a child. For example, my studies of stress-inducing factors among children have indicated that "getting up in front of the class" is an incident that causes much concern and worry to a large number of children. It has been my experience that this condition also prevails with a large numbers of adults.

It has been clearly demonstrated that prolonged and unrelenting nervous tension developing from psychological stress can result in Psychosomatic disorders, which in turn can cause various serious diseases.

It should be mentioned that physiological and psychological conceptions of stress have evolved independently within their respective fields. One writer on the subject, Anis Mikhail, once proposed the following holistic definition of stress for the purpose of emphasizing the continuity between psychological and physiological theorizing, "Stress is a state which arises from an actual or perceived demand-capability imbalance in the organism's vital adjustment actions, and which is partially manifested by a nonspecific response."[8]

Social Stress

Human beings are social beings. They do things together. They play together. They work together for the benefit of society. They have fought together in time of national emergencies in order to preserve the kind of society in which they believe. This means that life involves a constant series of social interactions. These interactions involve a two-way street in that the individual has some sort of impact upon society, and in turn, society has an influence upon the individual. There are obviously many levels of social stress in life situations. For example, economic conditions and other social problems have been found to be very stressful for many people.

Negative attitudes about social interactions will almost always generate hard feelings and hostility among groups, making for more stressful conditions for all concerned. Also a neutral or *laissez faire* attitude often degenerates into one of tolerance, and as such, can become almost as devastating as a negative attitude. In fact, the development of an "I don't care" attitude can often make life intolerable and bring about stress. People themselves hold the key to avoidance of undesirable social stress in any kind of environment, and good social relationships are more likely to be obtained if one assumes a positive attitude in such relationships.

CAUSES OF STRESS

A fair question to raise might be, What doesn't cause stress? This is mentioned because most human environments, including the worksite and society as a whole, are now seen as being stress inducing to some degree. In recent years so many causes of cancer have been advanced that many persons have almost come to the conclusion that *everything* causes cancer. Perhaps the same could be said of stress. Because it has reached near epidemic proportions, it is easy to believe that *everything* causes stress.

Factors that induce stress are likely to be both general and specific. This means that certain major life events can be stress inducing. Also, in our day-to-day environments, many specific causes of stress can elevate undesirable stress levels.

A number of researchers have studied certain *life events* as causes of stress. They have attempted to find out what kinds of health problems are associated with various events, normal and abnormal, that afflict people either in the normal course of events or as a result of some sort of misfortune, such as "the death of a loved one."

As important as life events scales are as a means of determining causes of stress, some specialists feel that another good measure is that which is concerned with day-today problems. These are considered to be "daily hassles," such as "too many things to do."

EFFECTS OF STRESS

The viewpoint that prompted the comment "almost everything causes stress," could be applied with the assertion that "stress causes everything." A tragic consequence is that stress-related psychological and physiological disorders are viewed as primary social and health problems. Compelling evidence from studies and clinical trials, as well as many standard medical textbooks, attribute anywhere from 50 to 80 percent of all diseases at least in part to stress-related origins.

The literature by various medical authorities shows that among other conditions, the following in some way could be stress related: diabetes, cirrhosis of the liver, high blood pressure, peptic ulcer, migraine headaches, multiple sclerosis, lung disease, injury due to accidents, mental health problems, cancer, and coronary heart disease.

It is interesting to note that some recent findings suggest that stress can have an effect on the brain and memory. One report[9] showed that several days of exposure to high levels of the stress hormone cortisol can impair memory.

In his interesting book on this subject, J. Douglas Bremner[10] presented two main theories: (1) stress induced brain damage is responsible for a spectrum of trauma-related psychiatric disorders - making these disorders, in effect, the result of neurological damage and (2) stressors, acting through a depression of disruption of mental processes, can translate directly into an increased risk for poor health outcomes, including heart disease, cancer and infectious diseases.

Finally, a serious effect of stress, particularly for women, is that which is concerned with one's appearance. According to one source[11] "stress hormones and their effects can aggravate skin problems from excess oil to eczema, can mess with your stresses, and often have whole-body beauty consequences." In fact, stress can trigger just about every skin condition one can think of – sometimes in little as seconds (hives) or days (psoriasis). Although many dermatologists are not sure of the direct connection between stress and specific skin conditions, they agree that it does exist.

PERSONALITY AND STRESS

Before commenting on personality as it pertains to stress, it seems appropriate to briefly discuss my own conception of personality. Ordinarily, personality is often dealt with only as a psychological entity. I think of it in terms of a broad frame of reference, which is the *total* personality. I view this total personality as consisting of physical, social, emotional, and intellectual aspects. This conforms more or less with what has become a rather common description of personality – *existence as a person*, and this should be interpreted to mean the whole person or unified individual.

There appears to be general agreement that personality can influence how individuals handle stress. On the other hand, there is much less agreement regarding personality as a causal factor in disease. One specific example of this is the difference of opinion regarding the extent to which certain types of personality are associated with heart disease. A case in point is that which concerns the early work of Meyer Friedman and Ray H. Rosenman,[12] who designated Type A behavior and Type B behavior. A person with Type A behavior tends to be aggressive, ambitious, and competitive, and puts pressure on herself in getting things done. An individual with Type B behavior is more easy going, relaxed, and tends to have self-imposed pressure. With regard to these two types of behavior, the authors have commented, "In the absence of a Type A Behavior Pattern, coronary heart disease almost never occurs before 70 years of age, regardless of the fatty foods eaten, the cigarettes smoked or the lack of exercise. But when the behavior pattern is present, coronary heart disease can easily erupt in one's thirties and forties."

This point of view has been challenged by some, the main point of contention being that there is little in the way of solid objective evidence to support the hypothesis. In this regard it is interesting that many heart specialists have noted that death from heart disease is on a downward trend and may be expected to continue. They credit this, among other things, to diet, control of high blood pressure and particularly to exercise.

It is interesting to note that in a special symposium on the interaction between the heart and brain at an American Psychiatric Association meeting a few years ago, Rosenman reported that a 22-year research project found that Type As were twice as likely as Type Bs to develop coronary heart disease.[13] In addition, however, the highly competitive nature found in Type A people increases the likelihood that important warning signs of heart disease, such as chest pain, will be denied. It is estimated that Type As also survive better than Type Bs, and it is speculated that this may have something to do with Type As adeptness at denial. This is to say that once a heart attack has occurred, Type A people tend to deny their symptoms, and therefore may be better at suppressing the health anxieties that often accompany recovery from heart attack. According to Rosenman, with less anxiety there is less adrenaline release and a greater feeling of control over life.

In another frame of reference, Benjamin Newberry,[14] writing in my series, *Stress in Modern Society,* reported that Type As are highly susceptible to many stress responses, including hostility and aggression. It is suggested that the consequences of the Type A behavior pattern depend upon other aspects of personality and temperament. It is hypothesized that the Type A behavior pattern will be associated with dysphoric emotion and disease susceptibility in individuals who are high in reactivity (roughly, high in biological predisposition to introversion). The social environments of these people will have imposed the Type A behavior pattern on them despite its compatibility with their underlying temperament.

There is general agreement that one manifests her personality through certain behavior traits and characteristics. This being the case, if these traits and characteristics can be positively identified as being detrimental to one's health, it may be possible to modify behaviors that cause the problem. (Chapter 12 will discuss behavior modification in detail.)

Chapter 3

GENDER DIFFERENCES AND STRESS

Certain gender differences have various degrees of influence on how individuals confront the environment. The extent to which these differences are concerned with stress is likely to vary from one person to another. The reader should view the discussions in this chapter with this frame of reference in mind.

Are the various environments in which one has to operate more stressful for males or for females? The fact that this is not an easy question to answer is found in some of the conflicting literature on the subject. In general, it appears that the environment as a whole is more stressful for males than females up to about 12 years of age. However, after that time and long into adulthood practically all aspects of society are much more stressful for females than for males.

Gender-role stereotyping makes it incumbent on us to examine the whole area of gender differences. These differences are not only anatomical and physiological, but cultural, psychological, and sociological as well.

A starting point in the recognition of gender differences is that of the male and female reproductive structures, and although these differences are well-known to many, perhaps a review is in order, and this is the subject of the following discussion.

MALE REPRODUCTIVE STRUCTURES
AND THEIR FUNCTIONS

The male reproductive system is composed of the penis (the sensitive head of which is known as the glans); the urethra (the tube which extends from bladder to glans and through which urine and semen are passed); the seminal vesicles (semen storage place); the vas deferens (tube extending from the testicles); the epididymus (where sperm are stored and mature); and the testicles (which produce both sperm and male sex hormones).

When blood fills the spongy tissue of which the penis is composed, an erection occurs. The penis may become erect as a result of sexual excitation, a full bladder, irritation as from tight clothing, or even for no specific reason that the individual is aware of. Rhythmic movements of the penis within the vagina or a comparable close-fitting structure gives rise simultaneously to orgasm (neurological climax) and ejaculation (discharge of semen). (Most boys experience ejaculation at 12 or 13 years of age.) Orgasm and ejaculation may occur as a result of self-stimulation or during sleep. When it occurs during sleep, it is referred to as a nocturnal emission or a "wet dream."

Sperm are microscopic and are shaped like tadpoles. Their thrashing tails propel them about and are the means by which they move through the vagina and womb and into the Fallopian tubes where conception ordinarily takes place. Well over 250 million sperm cells may be present in a single ejaculation. The fluid which carries the sperm comes from the seminal vesicles and the prostate gland and is called semen.

The testicles or testes are carried outside the body in a sac, the scrotum; and they produce male sex hormones (androgen or testosterone) as well as sperm. It is this hormone that, as a result of stimulation of the testes by the "master" endocrine gland, the pituitary, gives rise to the appearance of the secondary sex characteristics at puberty.

A loose skin, the prepuce or foreskin surrounds the end of the penis. Sometimes this skin is removed ("circumcised") shortly after birth. Various reasons ranging from "health" to ritualistic tradition are given for this practice, but a vast majority of males in human history have survived without this operation.

FEMALE REPRODUCTIVE
STRUCTURES AND THEIR FUNCTIONS

The external sexual parts of the female are the lips or labia (the labia majora and within them the labia minora). Within the labia are located, from the top to bottom, the clitoris, the urinary opening and the vaginal opening, inside which lies the vaginal tract where the penis is inserted during intercourse and into which sperm are deposited. The cervix or lower end of the womb (uterus) projects into the vagina at its far end. Fallopian tubes (oviducts) lead from the uterus to the ovaries.

The female clitoris is the counterpart of the male penis. It is quite small (from less than one-fourth inch to one-half inch in length) but extremely sensitive to stimulation. Moreover, it has a glans, a foreskin and in some females is capable of erection. Its stimulation is an important aspect of female sexual excitement; but distension of the vagina by the penis is also an important aspect of sexual excitement, at least in some females.

To some females the orgasm is a climactic event very much like that of the male. Others seem to find no less satisfaction in a different, less violent and perhaps more prolonged climax. Still others enjoy the sexual experience without ever identifying a climax or orgasm as such. It has been suggested that since it apparently does not exist in females of other species the female orgasm is a purely human invention – by no means experienced by all human females. This information is of importance because many females feel that they are somehow inadequate if they do not reach a certain kind of climax. Indications are that unlike males, females are capable of a considerable range of natural variability in this respect.

The uterus is a pear-shaped structure in which the embryo grows until birth. Its lining, the endometrium elaborates both the menstrual material and, if conception takes place, a portion of the placenta. The embryo is attached to the placenta by the umbilical cord; and the placenta serves as an organ of interchange between mother and embryo. That is, nutrients pass from mother to child and waste materials pass from child to mother for elimination. However, there is no intermingling of the blood of child and mother; nor are there nerve connections between the two.

The ovaries are the female sex glands and are analogous to the male testes. They produce eggs (ova) and also, like the testes, secrete hormones. The female sex hormone, estrogen, actually includes a number of closely related hormones, and is responsible for the typically feminine secondary sexual characteristics which tend to become prominent beginning at puberty. A second major hormone, progesterone, is produced by the ovaries if conception occurs. This hormone then brings about change in the body which adjusts it for child bearing. For example, the uterus prepares to hold and nourish the embryo, the breasts make ready to produce milk, and menstruation and ovulation (the releasing of an egg from the ovary) cease, with the result that additional conception cannot take place during pregnancy.

The Menstrual Cycle

During the years between puberty and menopause, the female undergoes a monthly (plus or minus a few days) cycle of events which, in effect, represent repeated efforts of the body to ready itself for child bearing. The cycle can be described as beginning with a gradual building up by the uterine wall of a rich supply of blood. Presently, ovulation occurs (an ovary expels an egg) and an egg is propelled towards the uterus via a Fallopian tube. If a sperm reaches and penetrates the egg on this journey, conception has thereby occurred; and the fertilized egg moves on into the uterus and lodges in the "built up" wall where it begins the process of growth into a child. If this occurs, the fertilized egg, like a seed sprouting roots, becomes attached to the wall of the uterus; and the medium of interchange between mother and embryo, the placenta, is formed. (Following birth, the placenta is discharged – the "afterbirth.") On the other hand, if conception does not occur, the egg disintegrates, and the lining of the wall of the uterus is discharged from the body as in the menstrual flow.

Menstruation begins approximately 14 days after ovulation, lasts for four to six days, and then a new build-up of the uterine wall begins. This 14-day period between ovulation and the coming menstruation tends to be relatively stable in females. However, the number of days between ovulation and the last menstruation tends to vary markedly, depending upon the number of days in the particular female's total cycle. Thus, if a female has a 28-day period between the ending of one menstrual period and the beginning of the next, ovulation can be expected in the middle of the period – 14 days after one menstrual period and the beginning of the next. However, if a female has a 34-day lapse between periods, since the 14 days between ovulation and the coming menstruation tends to be constant – 34 minus 14 or 20 represents the number from last menstruation and to the coming ovulation. Obviously, calculating when a female will be fertile (perhaps for a period of about 12 to 48 hours per month) requires an ability to predict with accuracy when the next coming menstruation will begin. Such knowledge of any female menstrual cycle cannot ordinarily be acquired without at least a year's careful logging of the onsets of menstruation. Some females are so irregular that accurate calculation of ovulation is not possible. Some cycles are so short that ovulation occurs during menstruation. At any rate, an accurate knowledge of the individual female's pattern of menstrual cycles is required for predicting when conception is possible, whether a "safe period" or pregnancy is being sought.

A number of additional points of interest are associated with the menstrual cycle. Following are several: (1) Cycles that are ordinarily regular may become irregular or periods may be skipped entirely due to stress, illness or no apparent reason; (2) Unlike lower animals, the human female does not tend to experience maximum sexuality (called estrus or "in heat" in animals) during ovulation. Rather her sexual interest is likely to be greatest just before or just after menstruation; (3) Females sometimes are irritable or nervous shortly after menstruation. They and their mates should certainly be aware of this fact; (4) Many females experience mild to severe pains (dysmenorrhea) before and/or during menstruation. Occasionally the cause is organic, but often it is unknown. Sometimes it is apparently due to psychological factors; (5) The female should not regard herself as an invalid during menstruation. Most should continue to do what they are used to doing, including bathing and being physically active. However, they should avoid such things as exceptionally heavy exercise and going into unusually cold water.

A long negative tradition has tended to put the phenomenon of menstruation in an evil light. At one time the solar center of a woman's universe was her uterus, and monthly menstrual cycles precipitated great storms of disorders – throbbing lust, hysteria, and insanity.[1] It is not commonly called the "curse" anymore. ("The curse of Eve.") Nor so often thought of as being "sick." Still, because of a lack of education and guidance, the onset of menstruation is a severely traumatic experience to an unreasonably large number of teenage girls. At best, it is regarded as a nuisance by most females. However, mature individuals are likely to view it as a necessary condition of being a female – a basic aspect of femininity and an important factor in self-understanding and self-acceptance as a woman.

OTHER GENDER DIFFERENCES

When entering the world, the male child comes in with some degree of fanfare – "*It's a Boy*!!!" The female more often than not is likely to get a more suppressed announcement. "You have a little girl." Expectations are likely to be much loftier for males – "Maybe he will grow up to be president." I have yet to hear this said of a baby girl.

Interestingly enough, immediately after they are born we seem to relegate girls to somewhere between second and third class citizenship by dressing them in "pink" and boys in "blue." If the reader will indulge me while I delve into the field of color psychology with a bit of wild speculation perhaps I can explain. In certain kinds of competition first place is designated by a blue ribbon, second place, by a red ribbon, and third place, by a white ribbon. Thus, do we automatically declare boy babies *winners* over girl babies at the outset by garbing them in blue and by placing girls somewhere between second and third place – pink being a combination of red and white?

In any case, from a growth and developmental point of view, while at birth the female is from one-half to one centimeter less in length than the male and around 300 grams less in weight, she is actually a much better developed organism. It is estimated that on average at the time of entrance into school, the female is usually six to 12 months more physically mature than the male. As a result, girls tend to learn earlier how to perform such tasks of manual dexterity as buttoning their clothing. In one of my own observational studies of preschool children some years ago, it was found that little girls were able to perform the task of tying their shoe laces at a rate of almost four times that of little boys.

Due to certain hormonal conditions, boys tend to be more aggressive, restless, and impatient. In addition, the male has more rugged bone and muscular structure and, as a consequence, greater strength than that of the female at all ages. Because of this, males tend to display greater muscular reactivity which in turn expresses itself in a stronger tendency toward restlessness and vigorous activity. This condition is concerned with the greater oxygen consumption required to fulfill the male's need for increased energy production.

In the area of basic skill performances between males and females, beginning with the basic locomotor skill of running, little difference occurs in performance of boys and girls of elementary school age. However, after that time boys increase their speed and endurance at a rate greater than the increase among girls. Although this may be true on the average, it must be recognized that many girls become excellent performers in distance running. For example, three decades ago it would have been outside the realm of general acceptance that women would be capable of effectively running a Marathon. Recently, world-class female Marathoners regularly are timed in what would have been credible performance for males in the past.

In the skill of jumping there are many levels in performance for children. Generally speaking, they tend to improve their performance as they get older. This improvement tends to be more pronounced for boys.

In the propulsion skills, especially throwing, gender differences in the performance level among children substantially favors boys. At all age levels, boys are generally better at throwing for distance than girls, but there is not such a pronounced gender difference in throwing for accuracy.

It is conceivable that the male organism might be compared to an engine which operates at higher levels of speed and intensity that the less energetic female organism. Over three decades ago in a conversation, my friend and contemporary, the late Franklin Henry of the University of California at Berkeley, told me that he had found in his research that males have what might be termed an "active response set" whereas females, a "reactive response set." This could be interpreted to mean that males confront the environment with an activity orientation while females have a response orientation.

Another factor to take into account is the difference in Basal Metabolic Rate (BMR) in young boys and girls. The BMR is indicative of the speed at which body fuel is changed into energy, as well as how fast this energy is used. BMR can be measured in terms of calories per meter of body surface with a calorie representing a unit measure of heat energy in food. It has been found that on average BMR rises from birth to about three years of age and then starts to decline until the ages of approximately 20 to 24. The BMR is higher for boys than for girls. Because of the higher BMR, boys in turn will have a higher amount of energy to expend. Because of differences in sex hormonal conditions and BMR, it appears logical to assume that these factors will influence the male in his behavior patterns.

Some studies have shown that as far as hyperactivity is concerned, boys may outnumber girls by a ratio of as much as nine to one. This may be the reason why teachers generally tend to rate young males as being so much more aggressive than females with the result that young boys are considered to be more negativistic and extraverted. Because of these characteristics, boys generally have poorer relationships with their teachers than do girls, and in terms of behavior problems and discipline in the age range from five to nine, boys account for twice as many disturbances as girls. The importance of this factor is borne out when it is considered that good teacher-pupil relationships tend to raise the achievement levels of both sexes.

Various studies have shown that girls generally receive higher grades than boys despite the fact that boys may achieve as well, and in some instances, better than girls. It is also clearly evident that boys in the early years fail twice as often as girls even when there is no significant differences between intelligence and achievement test scores of both sexes. This suggests that even though both sexes have the same intellectual tools, there are other factors that militate against learning as far as boys are concerned.

Although all of this may be true for preteen boys, the situation seems to change for girls after about 13 years of age. After that time many aspects of society become anxiety-provoking for girls. This is especially true of the school environment. Research in recent years on this subject can be summarized as follows:

1. There is little encouragement for girls to pursue mathematics and science.
2. There are subtle teacher practices, such as calling on boys more often or gearing school activities more to the males.
3. Boys call out answers eight times more often than girls. When boys call out, teachers are more apt to listen.
4. When boys do not answer, teachers seem more likely to encourage them to give answers or opinions than they are to encourage girls.
5. Girls are at a disadvantage in taking tests because such tests may be geared to male performance. Taking this into account some standard intelligence tests now have a masculinity-femininity index.
6. Although there does not appear to be much difference in test anxiety between boys and girls, at the same time girls are prone to suffer more stress over report cards than do boys.
7. Teachers appear to encourage male students to work with laboratory equipment moreso than they do girls.
8. Vocational education programs are often geared to boys in spite of the fact that a large percentage of the work force is female.
9. Stereotypical images still appear in textbooks, with an overwhelming number of male authors and role models studied in class.

(Some school systems are attempting to correct some of these conditions by inaugurating *gender equity* programs.)

All of the above, as well as other conditions, make for serious stress-inducing factors for junior and senior high school girls. In addition to a stressful school environment, there are other female teenage behaviors that suggest that girls suffer more stress than boys.

One study[2] examined gender differences in established measures of shyness, sociability, loneliness, and hopelessness among approximately 1,900 adolescent smokers and non-smokers. It was determined that gender significantly interacted with smoking status (current smoker vs. non-smoker) in this sample of adolescents. There were several interesting differences between gender-smoking status groups. For example, male smokers had elevated scores on loneliness and hopelessness, when compared to female smokers and non-smokers of both genders. Also, female smokers scored significantly lower on shyness than male smokers, female non-smokers, and male non-smokers.

In another study[3] motivations for drug use considered to be dysfunctional were reported by females more often than by males.

As far as *suicide* is concerned, results of one study[4] indicated that 32.1 percent of 561 high school students questioned, had seriously thought of attempting suicide during the past 12 months. Positive responses by females were significantly higher than males (38.6 percent and 25.5 percent respectively). Positive responses by females in grade 9 (41.2 percent) and 10 (54.2 percent) were significantly higher than males and females in other grades. A total of 19.9 percent indicated that they had made a specific plan about how to attempt suicide within the last 12 months. A significantly higher number of females (23.9 percent) over males (15.9 percent) had made suicide plans. In comparing both grades and gender, 10th grade girls (36.9 percent) were significantly more likely to make suicide plans. Seven percent of all respondents said they had attempted suicide during the past 12 months. Females in grade 9 (11.6 percent) and 10 (16.9 percent) were significantly more likely to attempt suicide than any other group. It was concluded that the most susceptible population in teen suicide were 9th and 10th grade girls and educators should become familiar with indicators of suicide behaviors so that timely intervention may be possible.

As far as gender differences in stress in *older* women is concerned, some interesting information is available. A serious stressor among some older women is one of *financial worries.* About twice as many women as men cite this to be a source of stress for them. Moreover, this is the case of the so-called "well-to-do" women as well as those with low and average incomes. They seem to be concerned as to whether or not they will have enough money to "see them through."

In this general regard the following interesting information was reported at a meeting of the Older Women's League:

- Despite the "myth of the wealthy elderly," the nation's women of age 65 or older fare worse economically than their male counterparts.
- In general, older women are poorer, those who work have worse jobs, are paid less, have worse pensions and worse medical coverage and are more obligated to care for family members who are ill or disabled.

- Older women are less likely to reap the economic benefits from a lifetime of work and they are more likely to live in poverty and isolation.
- Rather than being cared for, they are likely to continue to sacrifice their health and their livelihood to care for others.
- About 15 percent of older women fall below the government's official poverty line. The figure for older men is less than half as high.
- On the average if women become widowed, divorced or separated in old age or if they are already single, they lack resources and health and pension benefits equal to those of men.
- As one example of financial income, a typical male in the age range of 65-69 averages 27 percent more in social security benefits than a typical woman in the same age range. As far as pension benefits are concerned males average more than 45 percent more per month than do women.

Generally speaking, according to this report there is ample reason for the average older woman to consider financial problems as a serious source of stress.

In an interesting report several years ago, Sandra Levy[5] reviewed findings that supported the conclusion that adult women across all age categories are more distressed than their male counterparts although the source of this distress may differ for middle-age and older women cohorts. Underlying the disturbances for the middle-aged women are role loss, lack of marketable skills and general ability to "break into" the larger social arena. For elderly women the key issue underlying mood and behavioral dysfunction is identified as social isolation.

A point that needs to be raised at this time is the susceptibility to stress between males and females. As we know, the condition of stress is a highly individualized, subjective perception. Nevertheless, the following question should be raised: Is there a commonality of stressors to which women are uniquely susceptible? To this question, the consensus is no doubt affirmative, as is the judgment that such stressors have multiplied at a rate far in excess of those of their male counterparts. This is attributed in large measure to radical changes in societal norms which have attended women's suffrage, the feminist movement, dramatic rates of divorce, increased geographical mobility, discontinuity in extended family relationships, and a steady influx of women into occupations and professions, previously the proprietary interest of males.

Among the negative consequences of such radical cultural transformations in the role of women have been disturbing qualitative and quantitative changes in illness patterns and increased incidence of life-threatening diseases. in fact, I have found that stress is causing more women than ever to consult their doctors; 50 percent of female office visits are said to be stress-related, and twice as many women as men make such office visits.

For several years some writers have suggested that there are signs that women's vulnerability increases as fast as their independence. It was once contended that over a century ago, peptic ulcers were a woman's ailment, by a ratio of seven to three. Then as frontier rigors were replaced by industrial ones, life got easier for women, and harder for men, and, from 1929 to 1940, nine out of ten victims were male. But since mid-20th century the incidence of ulcers of women was again on the rise.[6]

Almost three decades ago an interesting point of view was expressed by Marianne Frankenhaeuser[7] of the Experimental Psychology Research Unit of the Swedish Medical Research Council. She suggested that women do not have the same readiness as do men in responding to environmental demands by adrenaline release. She did not feel that this response was due to sex, but more to a behavior pattern, that is common to men in Western society.

A study of gender individual differences in stress reactivity among college students is one that was conducted by Joy Humphrey and George Everly.[8] They used a "State Measurement Scale" for the purpose of finding out from male and female college students how they generally felt while experiencing a stress response situation. In other words, the purpose was to investigate the perceptual dimensions of stress reactions in males and females.

The study showed that males and females "perceive" different stress reactions. Of greatest disparity between the perceptions of males and females was the emergence of *gastrointestinal sensitivities* (such as upset stomach) exclusively among males and the emergence of an *aversive affective sensitivity* (such as feeling "high strung") exclusively among females.

The investigators felt that it was impossible to attribute any significance to the appearance of gastrointestinal sensitivity among males and an aversive affective sensitivity among females. However, they did speculate that sociocultural factors may have been involved. The reason for this is that it may be socially acceptable for males to develop "executive ulcers." Regarding the aversive affective sensitivity, generally speaking, males are taught to repress emotion, and many males perceive such emotion to be a sign of weakness. Similarly, females have been traditionally taught that it is appropriate for them to demonstrate emotion. If cultural factors do indeed influence perceptions of responsiveness, one might be willing to speculate that, eventually there would be more homogeneous perceptions of stress reactions among males and females. (Incidentally, I replicated this study recently and found essentially the same results after more than two decades.)

Another point of view indicating that women could be more stressed out than men is based on their prescription drug consumption. Psychotic drug prescriptions for females are twice as high as those for males, but the reason for this is not clear. One possibility is that women with emotional problems may be much more likely to consult a physician and also much more apt to admit that they are suffering from such difficulties than men. On the other hand, epidemiologic studies suggest that members of the so-called "weaker sex" are indeed much more prone to anxiety and depressive disorders. Feminists counter that the reason for this is that women are exploited in society and are therefore bound to suffer greater stress, which is mistakenly assumed by the (often male) doctors to produce intrinsic nervous instability. If this were true, one would suspect the female doctors evaluating patients of their own sex would be more sympathetic and not reach for the prescription pad so readily.

It has been suggested that just the opposite may occur. Women with nervous symptoms are more likely to have hypnotic tranquilizers prescribed when they consult female physicians. There could be a reason for this. For example, because female physicians may be more sympathetic and understanding, they are able to diagnose anxiety states more accurately and frequently.[9]

Finally, the gender difference of longevity. On average women can expect to live more than five years longer than men. There are different explanations for this. We do know that heart disease and cancer, leading causes of death, tend to kill more men than women. Although we are not quite sure of the reason for this, one source[10] suggests that it could have to do with the different ways men and women handle stress (which might make some diseases worse) or maybe with the way hormones work in men's and women's bodies.

Chapter 4

FEMALE SEXUALITY AND STRESS

The need to learn to think in new ways about old things has been accompanied by a new awareness of the range of ways if which human beings can behave – sexually and otherwise. It is hoped that this new awareness plus greater knowledge and understanding of human needs will lead, in time, to patterns of sexual behavior that will be conducive to greater human happiness and fulfillment.

By way of perspective, it is interesting to know that our American sexual behavior, our ideas of sexual morality, our laws and extramarital and marital customs, derive from two major sources, historically speaking. For the most part, our sexual morality and laws originated among the ancient Jews (recorded in the Old Testament, for example, Leviticus), were picked up almost entirely by the Christian church, and were transmitted northward through Europe, to England and thence to America. This is the historical background behind our strong feelings, and in some cases severe laws, concerning sexuality. Times have changed, but have we always changed with them? It was Albert Einstein who once said something to the effect that everything has changed in recent years except our ways of thinking about them.

Such is pretty much the case as far as sexuality is concerned in modern times. Our ways of thinking about such things as dating, courtship, sex, and marriage tend automatically to follow along traditional lines in spite of the fact that modern circumstances are in many ways vastly different from what they were in the past. For example, it is still claimed by some that "woman's place is in the home." But is this reasonable in a society which has discovered that educated women can do virtually everything that men can do in the world of work? Is it necessarily true in a society where girls receive the same education as boys and in many cases decide that their greatest hope for happiness and self-fulfillment lies in science, or in business – rather than tending to the chores of housekeeping and child rearing, for which domestic work they may very well receive no training at all? Not only have times changed, but they are in the process of changing now, perhaps more rapidly than ever before.

COMPONENTS OF SEXUALITY

The whole area of sexuality is so broad in scope that it simply cannot be dealt with only in terms of "the quality of being sexual," a standard dictionary definition of the term. Indeed, sexuality needs to be thought of in terms of comprehensiveness. In fact, my distinguished colleague at the University of Maryland, Jerrold S. Greenberg, writing in my series *Stress in Modern Society*[1] identified four specific sexuality components as being cultural, psychological, biological, and ethical. Let us consider this premise.

The *cultural* component of sexuality includes historical influences, intimate relationships (dates, marriage partners, friends), and all the sexually-related customs we learn from people in our environment. This component is the sum of cultural influences upon our sexual thoughts and actions. In our society, these cultural influences include radio, television, films, advertisements, and literature. One need only look at the shelves of bookstores or videotape rental shops, read magazine advertisements for liquor, tobacco, or automobiles, note the films playing in local theaters, or listen to popular music on the radio to realize how pervasive sexual cultural influences are in contemporary American society.

The *psychological* component of sexuality includes our thoughts and how comfortable we are with our sexual selves. Some of us learned that sexual topics, were taboo, sexual behaviors immoral, and sexual fantasies perverse. Some of us learned this at a very early age, either explicitly or incidentally. For example, young children naturally explore their genitals; it feels good to them. Parents who find this behavior embarrassing or who believe it to be wrong will admonish the child for such behavior. The child learns that deriving pleasure from his or her genitals is wrong. However, even more subtle learning about sexuality occurs. What do you think the message is when the family conversations include such a wide range of topics that the omission of sexual ones is evident? Or, when a sister's beginning of menstruation is "hush hush?" Or, when birth control is never discussed in a family with teenage children? That these topics are off limits conveys the message that sexual thoughts and actions are wrong and bad;

and if you have any of these thoughts, you are bad too. Since nearly everyone has a sexual desire or sexual fantasy or has touched his or her genitals at some time, it can be readily seen that the potential exists for a lot of distressed people in our society.

The *biological* component is probably the one first thought of when sexuality is the topic. This component includes one's physiological response to sexual stimulation, the biology of reproduction, puberty, physical changes as a result of pregnancy, physical changes associated with aging that affect sexual function, and the like. Perceptions of sexuality, for example, anxiety associated with moral judgment regarding particular sexual behaviors, can interfere with normal biological functioning.

The *ethical* component of sexuality involves our judgments of what is right and what is wrong, what is good and what is bad, about sexual topics. We are influenced by our moral judgments, by past experience, by important adults in our youth, and by our religious views. In a changing society such as ours, these moral judgments are often called into question. Is abortion moral? If so, under what circumstances? Is premarital or extramarital sex moral? Is the use of contraceptives right? Is the trend for mothers of young children to work outside the home good? When components of our society change, the lack of societal consensus on societal moral issues becomes stressful for us. Furthermore, these moral issues influence other components of our sexuality. Disagreements on moral issues can have a negative impact on our relationships with other people, can lead to guilt and shame, and can result in difficulty with normal sexual physiology.

SEXUAL DISCRIMINATION

Discrimination of any kind whether it is racial, ethnic, or sexual, can be very stressful for those victimized by it.

Women have been discriminated against in many ways; in relation to men they have been placed in subordinate roles. For example, "woman" means the "wife of man" and the implication could be that there is no such thing as a woman separate from wifehood. During their reproductive years women were often pregnant and occupied in caring for children, and this simply meant that men have been in a position to work out social arrangements that fit masculine wishes and needs.

In the sexual field, throughout recorded history women have been more discriminated against than men. In years past in prostitution the legal penalties have typically been assessed against women. They have been the one prosecuted rather than men. Under the double standard the female has been severely faulted for the same sexual behavior for which the male achieved recognition from other males. Generally, not nearly such strong demands for virginity have been placed on males as opposed to females. In many instances of rape cases the woman had to prove her sexual virtue, and if she had violated conventionality in any way, the man could go free. This approach is now changing. Traditionally, the penalties for adultery have been much more severe for women than for men. Also a menstruating woman was considered "unclean." Even in the New Testament this un-cleanliness existed for seven days after menstruation, and anything she touched sat on, or lay on became unclean. If any man had intercourse with her, he was unclean for seven days also.

According to custom the female should be appropriately ignorant concerning sex. Her concern was in establishing a relationship; one of her main objectives was "to hook a man." Since women were supposed to be innocent and before marriage sexually initiated themselves, they sometimes expressed the desire to marry a sexually experienced man. Males were expected to be interested in the genital aspect of sex and, through prior experience, would know what to do. In this way female naivete would be both appreciated and overcome at the same time. The double standard accepted this as a legitimate distinction between male and female behavior. For the men, however, it gave them freedom to experiment sexually without being severely criticized. Although many of these inequalities still exist, women are now protesting them – asserting, even demanding their rights. Once this is achieved it will surely be to the advantage of both sexes.

STRESSORS OF SEXUAL ACTIVITY

It seems appropriate to begin the discussion of sexual activity with some comments about *masturbation* because the guilty feeling associated with this form of sexual activity can be extremely stressful for those who engage in it.

Masturbation, perhaps more accurately termed sexual self-stimulation, is a very common behavior among both males and females during the course of growing up. Incidentally, as far as the latter are concerned, it is interesting to note that "some 19th century English physicians cured masturbation with *clitorectomies* (removal of the clitoris). The 'thrill' (orgasm) for sake of the 'thrill,' especially among young females was socially abhorrent. It was wicked. It was barbaric."[2]

In spite of the long tradition of opinion to the contrary, there is no evidence that it is harmful, physiologically speaking. But psychologically, it can be devastating. This is because by various means, frequently unspoken, parents and others convey to the infant and child the impression that there is something profoundly wrong about so much as unnecessarily touching the genitals, let alone intentionally stimulating them. When the genitals are touched, as in urinating one is admonished to scrub the hands carefully because this part of the body has come to be thought of as dirty and germ ridden in spite of frequently bathing. Of course, under modern circumstances of living the genital region may actually be one of the cleanest parts of the body, and the urine of healthy people is harmless.

The pressure of long tradition which tends to put masturbation in the darkest possible light is not sufficient to prevent or stop masturbation in most healthy young people, but it is quite sufficient to give rise to severe guilt reactions in those who do it, which is to say most young people. Thus, as in the case in so many "symptoms" of childhood and youth, the problem gets its start not in the behavior itself but in the minds, facial expressions, and other responses of adults.

The major reason why masturbation has been given a "bum rap" is that certain conceptions about it have developed over the centuries. It began with the story of Onan in the Book of Genesis in the Old Testament. The widow of Onan's brother had no male children and Onan's father instructed him to personally remedy that oversight. Onan objected by "wasting his seed." The Lord smote Onan for this indiscretion and masturbation came to be known as Onanism. Christian morals were influenced greatly by Jewish codes of behavior and consequently, masturbation was condemned by Christian laws as well. Little wonder that the vestiges of this attitude are still with us (for example, the firing of Surgeon General Joycelyn Elders in 1994 for her "untimely" remarks of this subject.)

The following discussions will take into account various aspects of sexual activity, particularly those that are of concern to women.

Although all women are not stressed in the same manner by sexual activity, there are certain generalities that can be reported in this regard.

Commenting in my series on *Stress in Modern Society,* M. Lawrence Furst and Donald E. Morse[3] asserted that even with the so-called sexual revolution many women are still mired in the Victorian era in their sexual thinking and behavior. Although most mothers do not encourage premarital sexual relations for their daughters, premarital sex has increased greatly. Of the women born prior to 1900, three out of four were virgins before marriage. And as long ago as the 1970s three out of four had had premarital sex. (Incidentally, throughout history "sexual activity was confined to the institution of marriage and had been ordained by God for the purpose of the continuation of the species.")[4]

The feeling of guilt accompanying premarital sex is another potential stressor. Nevertheless, there is evidence that these feelings do not prevent some women from engaging in premarital sexual activities, and generally the guilt feelings lessen in time.

A major stressor for women about to have sexual intercourse for the first time is the fear that it will be painful. Although this varies among women, even with an intact hymen, if time is allowed for the onset of adequate natural lubrication, penetration usually causes only slight pain and bleeding.

Another cause for stress is related to the time needed for some women to become sexually aroused. Some women can become stressed if sufficient foreplay is lacking. In the same frame of reference it can be stressful for women to have a male partner with the "Speedy Gonzalez" syndrome; that is, when the male partner is "done" before his female partner has "started." Such an experience can cause no end of stress for some women.

Although it is not a concern for all women, another potential stressor for some of them is the question of whether to engage in extramarital sex. At one time not too long ago the sport of "wife swapping" (swinging) was popular among some couples. Perhaps this was an attempt to legitimize extramarital sex. In any case, extramarital affairs are probably on the decline because of the fear of AIDS, genital herpes, and other sexually transmitted diseases.

STRESS AND PREGNANCY

Writing in my series on *Stress in Modern Society,* John Sullivan and Joyce Cameron Foster[5] suggested that human pregnancy is a unique state in which the phenomenon of stress may be examined. Pregnancy is a time-limited experience in which there are enormous physical and psychological adjustments and changes (stresses). As the fetus grows and puts an increasing physiological load on the pregnant woman, the pregnancy process constitutes a "natural stress experience."

In addition, there is the experiential response of the woman and her partner. The amount of psychological stress during the pregnancy is a function of many factors: (1) personal, family, and cultural beliefs, perceptions, and expectations; (2) prior response patterns to stress and illness; (3) the extent of life stresses currently or recently experienced; (4)

perceived and actual coping abilities; and (5) response to the physical/psychological changes of pregnancy. The vulnerability of the human organism to symptoms/illness during the pregnancy process is probably related to the total load of both physical and psychological stress. At the very least, the quality of the pregnancy experience is affected.

In one extensive study,[6] the theory was developed that stress interacted with several other variables but more prominently with symptom proneness-resistance. Measures of stress, symptom proneness and minor pregnancy symptoms were developed to operationalize a model of the general theory on 1,315 pregnant women. Two models of stress were formulated: (1) stress as a pure motivational variable that energized latent behavior tendencies; and (2) stress with stimulus properties that elicited stress-related behaviors. The first theory predicted the symptoms of pregnant women in the first trimester, the second theory predicted the symptoms of the third trimester. It was concluded that as the adaptive range of the individual narrows, the increased load of stress acts as an elicitor. In the lower ranges of adaptability, stress acts with properties of a purely motivational variable. Path analyses were constructed for each month from the third to ninth month of pregnancy. Since the path weights changed during this period, descriptions of the process of pregnancy in terms of stress, symptom proneness, and psychological upset were provided as these related to minor pregnancy symptoms.

The earliest stressor of pregnancy for some women is the missed "first period." Depending upon the attitude toward pregnancy, this can bring forth either extreme joy or depression. Once pregnancy begins, "morning sickness" can be quite stressful.

Although increased levels of female hormones play a major role, pathological vomiting during pregnancy can be psychologically induced with pregnant women having several severe social stressors. Pregnancy gingivitis (swollen inflamed gums) is also said to be related to pregnancy hormones and stress. Other potentially stressful early pregnancy manifestations are fatigue, sleepiness and excessive urination. The major event of the second trimester is the gradually enlarging waistline. This can be stressful and may induce temporary depression for the new mother, especially if she always was concerned with her figure. The expanding figure is, of course, normal, but since some women eat when they are under stress, this practice can lead to obesity following childbirth.

In the third trimester, stress can be related to the enlarging, painful breasts and the kicking infant. In addition, there can be back pains that interrupt sleep, and sexual activities are greatly interfered with. Other possible third trimester complications are toxemia and persistent elevated diastolic blood pressure, both of which may be stress related.

SEXUAL HARASSMENT

It is difficult to define, or even describe the term *sexual harassment.* Perhaps we could say that whether or not something is sexually harassing depends in a large measure upon degree, circumstances, environment and a host of other variables.

Sexual harassment is defined as a form of sex discrimination under Title VII of the Civil Rights Act of 1974. Harassment ranges from the blatant exchange or denial of promotion and raises based on sexual favors to a "hostile working environment," defined by the Supreme Court as one in which the harassment is "sufficiently severe or pervasive to alter the conditions of the victim's employment and create an abusive working environment."

The fact that this definition is not extensive enough is shown in comments by some writers on the subject. For example, my previously-mentioned collaborators M. Lawrence Furst and Donald R. Morse suggest that sexual harassment takes many forms. These include being directly asked to go to bed with a fellow employee or boss, being touched without one's consent, being given suggestions of physical intimacy by intonation or description, hearing vivid descriptions of one's anatomy by fellow employees or supervisors, being forced to listen to "off-color" remarks or jokes, being shown pornographic pictures or films, and being coerced into wearing "sexy" clothes (without previously being apprised of that condition of employment).

Under any circumstances sexual harassment can be a very threatening and stressful experience for many women not only on the job but in other environments as well. As a result of some forms of sexual harassment, some women have been known to suffer from such problems as migraine head-aches, gastrointestinal disorders, loss of self-esteem, fear, sense of helplessness, back and neck pains and depression.

Although sexual harassment is most often inflicted on women, men can be victims (some women delight in seeing a "shy guy" blush).

As mentioned, sexual harassment can take place in other environments as well as on the job. For example, at social gatherings, public places (especially elevators), schools, colleges and the military.

Colleges across the country are asking task forces to reexamine and restructure their sexual harassment policies. Most colleges' policies defining sexual harassment are similar to those of the Equal Employment Opportunity Commission, which covers everything from unwanted sexual solicitation, verbal harassment, comments about anatomy, dirty jokes and any unwanted repeated communication of a sexual nature. Although faculty members are sometimes involved, in most cases the problem is student harassment; that is, most students who complain about sexual harassment are doing so because of other students. Nationally, college officials estimate that about 25 percent of female students are the victims of some type of sexual harassment – more often than not, from other students.[7]

In an important decision in February 1992 the Supreme Court expanded protection against sex discrimination at the public school secondary level. For the first time, students who are victims of sexual harassment and other forms of sex discrimination have the right to be awarded money damages from schools who receive federal funds.

In the military sexual harassment has been a serious problem. For example, the United States Navy has been involved in a series of highly publicized incidents of sexual harassment and abuse. In 1989 a female midshipman (woman) at the United States Naval Academy was chained to a urinal and photographed by male midshipmen. Later in November 1991 an admiral was relieved from a prestigious job after he failed to act promptly on a complaint by a female aide that she was sexually harassed at a convention of naval aviators. Such episodes as these caused the Navy to change its behavior standards as of March 1, 1992.

This Navy policy states that members of the Navy and Marine Corps will be fired outright "on the first substantial incident" involving the following circumstances:

1. Threats or attempts to influence another's career or job to obtain sexual favors.
2. Offering rewards in exchange for sexual favors.
3. Physical contact of a sexual nature which, if charged as a violation of the Uniform Code of Military Justice, could result in punitive discharge.

The specific circumstances that would call for automatic dismissal on a first offense state that "An incident is substantiated if there has been a court-martial conviction or the commanding officer determines that sexual harassment has occurred." A service member would retain the legal right to contest his or her dismissal. Previously, commanders had the option of dismissing the most serious violators of anti-harassment rules, but dismissal was not required.

A more recent military sex scandal brought to light in February 2003 is that of the occurrence of rape and assault at the United States Airforce Academy. More than 50 cases of possible assaults on female cadets were reported over the past decade. And, there are probably numerous others that were never reported. The irony of the assaults is that the Academy has been accused of protecting male cadets who assault women – in some cases, bringing disciplinary action against female cadets who report the attacks.

This whole fiasco infuriated some members of Congress and Senator Wayne Allard of Colorado was quoted as saying, "It's outrageous what's been happening to women at the Academy. A woman is raped, and when she complains to authorities, it's the women who is penalized."[8]

For years, efforts to decrease the incidence of sexual harassment, particularly of women victims, were modest, at best. The major reason for this has been due to the reluctance of women to come forward when sexual harassment occurred because of fear of reprisals against them. However, all of that changed somewhat in October 1991 when Anita Hill, an articulate Law Professor from the University of Oklahoma, appeared at the confirmation hearing of Supreme Court nominee, Clarence Thomas. Miss Hill testified that Mr. Thomas had sexually harassed her when she worked for him at the Education Department and the Equal Employment Opportunity Commission. Mr. Thomas denied the allegations and it came down to a question of which person was more believable. Interestingly enough a survey of 100 judges found that by a ratio of two to one, they found Miss Hill more believable than Mr. Thomas.

The testimony itself was somewhat overshadowed by the insensitive treatment of Miss Hill by some members of the Judiciary Committee. In fact, the hearing was characterized by Senator Barbara Mikulski of Maryland as an *inquisition,* one meaning of which is "an investigation conducted with little regard for individual rights."

A large majority of women in America were infuriated by the proceedings and the fallout of the event has been a tremendous increase in the number of formal complaints of sexual harassment against corporate employers. Also, as a result of these hearings many employers began harassment sensitivity training and seminars for their employees.

Sexual Abuse

The two most serious forms of sexual abuse are *rape* and *incest.* The former is difficult to define because legal definitions of the term may vary from one state to another. For purposes here, rape will be considered to be "forcing one to engage in sexual intercourse or other sexual activities against his or her will." A common definition of the term incest is "sexual intercourse between persons so closely related that they are forbidden to marry."

Although sexual harassment may be embarrassing and humiliating, sexual abuse can be devastating and have a lifelong impact on the victim. In this regard, a study[9] reported here shows evidence of how child sexual abuse can have a stressful influence on collage-age women.

The primary purpose of this study was to examine the relationship between daily stressors and physical symptoms in college-age women with a childhood history of sexual abuse and women without a history of childhood sexual abuse. It was hypothesized that women with a history of childhood sexual abuse would be particularly susceptible to the effects of daily stressors on physical symptoms, and would show more covariation between daily stressors and physical symptoms, compared to women without a history of childhood sexual abuse.

Four hundred and ninety one female college students were screened for histories of childhood (before age 15) and adulthood (after age 15) contact sexual abuse. Of these participants, 18 women with a history of childhood sexual abuse were assigned to the stress abuse group, and 27 women with no history of childhood and adulthood sexual abuse were assigned to the nonabuse group. These women filled out self-report measures of daily hassles and physical symptoms for 28 consecutive days.

During the five days preceding a highly stressful day, women in the stress abuse group reported significantly more physical symptoms than during the five days preceding a day of low stress. For the nonabuse group, there were no significant differences in reported physical symptoms between high- and low-stress days.

The pattern of results for physical symptoms suggests that women with a history of childhood sexual abuse may be particularly susceptible to the effects of heightened daily stress, and may display this susceptibility in the report of physical symptoms.

SEX EDUCATION

Sex education has to do with the joyous appreciation of living; of oneself as a special person; and of relationships with other people in families, in school, and with one's friends. It means learning respect for other persons as human beings and the importance of getting along with each other. It means understanding that all living things grow and reproduce, how mothers and fathers take care of their babies, that good health practices make for good health, how the body functions, what changes to expect when one's body grows, and that some individuals grow differently or more slowly. It means learning to tell the difference between what is helpful and what is harmful to people, making responsible decisions about one's own behavior, and making the most of one's best capabilities as a human being.

Much education in sexual attitudes and values takes place at home – some good, some not so good – long before children come to school. Parents continue to be the most crucial educational force as long as children are under their influence. As children grow, more sex education is given by peers both in school and outside the classroom. The classroom provides the more formal setting for guided discussions of whatever content has approval of parents and teachers. The neighborhood, the community, the church, the social class and the cultures in which children live all add their own special dimension.

The school deals with its part by first developing a sound sequential program that deals with basic understandings appropriate to the early grades. These basic understandings provide a foundation for more complex learnings in the later grades as children grow and develop. This program, unlike a mathematics curriculum, will be more readily accepted if it is developed by teachers and parent representatives together.

To develop such a program parents and teachers first need to know what children are learning from a variety of sources to which they are exposed. Second, they need to know what children *want* to know as the most effective teaching comes from this. Third, they should have identified what children may *need* to know for a good start toward healthy attitudes and behavior in the realm of sex and in the broader sense, of human sexuality.

A program should be designed to follow children's interests and to answer their questions rather than to initiate them. This being the case, parents have the opportunity to respond to their children's questions before they come up at school.

Sex education in the schools can be a great experience for students, parents and teachers, but it needs to be thoroughly planned, reviewed by a group that is broadly representative of the community, approved by a majority of parents, and taught by qualified teachers. Such a program can help boys and girls understand themselves, become wholesome individuals, and mark another step toward maturity.

At the present time, antisex-education forces are not so vigorously at work as they used to be on a national scale, but they are far from inactive. Where sex education has been initiated or continued, school personnel can expect to meet challenges at any time. Also, whenever children and youth are involved in some publicized sexual episode such as the raping of a classmate, the antisex-education people tend to blame the event or situation on school sex education and its arousing effects on the students. This can occur even though it is well known that such things can always happen, whether or not there have been sex education programs in the schools.

The overall trend of the times is in the direction of greater openness about sex. Accurate information is increasingly available to virtually all who want it. The language taboo is not nearly so strong. Mass media are available to deal directly with many aspects of the subject and, even within families where there was the least talk about sex, there is now oftentimes reasonably comfortable discussion of some aspects of the subject.

Vulnerable as they are to public pressure, it is hard to imagine the schools not following the general trend toward greater objectivity, openness and direct dealing with new knowledge as is expected in all other subject areas.

Chapter 5

DEALING WITH EMOTIONS

In introducing the subject of emotion, one is confronted with the fact that, for many years, it has been a difficult concept to define and, in addition, there have been many changing ideas and theories as far as the study of emotion is concerned. Obviously, it is not the purpose of a book of this nature to attempt to go into any great depth on a subject that has been one of the most intricate undertakings of psychology for many years. However, a general overview of the subject appears to be in order to help the reader have a clearer understanding of the emotional aspect of personality, particularly with regard to its involvement in stress.

Women have been emotionally stereotyped, perhaps unfairly, with such characterizations as "flighty," "high strung," "jumpy," and the like. Although it is said that women should be granted more latitude than men in expressing their emotions, at the same time it is supposed to be "unladylike" not to suppress an emotional pattern such as anger.

Emotional stress can be brought about by the stimulus of one of the emotional patterns. For example, the emotional pattern of anger can be stimulated by such factors as the thwarting of one's wishes, or a number of cumulative irritations. Response to such stimuli can be either *impulsive* or *inhibited.* An impulsive expression of anger is one that is directed against a person or an object, while the inhibited expressions are kept under control, and may be manifested by such overt behaviors as skin flushing.

Generally speaking, emotional patterns can be placed into the two broad categories of *pleasant* emotions and *unpleasant* emotions. Pleasant emotional patterns include such things as joy, affection, happiness, and love, while included among the unpleasant emotional patterns are anger, sorrow, jealousy, fear, and worry – an imaginary form of fear.

It is interesting to note that a good proportion of the literature is devoted to emotions that are unpleasant. In my analysis of several basic psychology books, much more space was given to such emotional patterns as fear, hate, and guilt, than to such pleasant emotions as love, sympathy, and contentment.

At one time or another all of us have manifested emotional behavior as well as ordinary behavior. Differences in the structure of the organism and in the environment will largely govern the degree to which individuals express emotional behavior. Moreover, the pleasantness of unpleasantness of an emotion seems to be determined by its strength or intensity, by the nature of the situation arousing it, and by the way the individual perceives or interprets the situation.

The ancient Greeks identified emotions with certain organs of the body. In general, sorrow was expressed from the heart (a broken heart); jealousy was associated with the liver; hate with the gall bladder; and anger with the spleen. In regard to the latter, we sometimes hear the expression "venting the spleen" on someone. This historical reference is made because in modern times we take into account certain conduits between the emotions and the body. These are by way of the *nervous* system and the *endocrine* system. The part of the nervous system that is principally concerned with the emotions is the *autonomic* nervous system, which controls functions such as heart rate, blood pressure, and digestion. When there is a stimulus of any of the emotional patterns, these two systems activate in the manner explained in Chapter 2. By way of illustration, if the emotional pattern of fear is stimulated, the heartbeat accelerates, breathing is more rapid, and blood pressure is likely to rise. Energy fuel is discharged into the blood from storage in the liver, which causes the blood sugar level to rise. These, along with other bodily functions, serve to prepare the person to cope with the condition caused by the fear. She then reacts with the "fight or flight" response, also discussed in Chapter 2.

When we attempt to evaluate the emotional aspect of personality, we encounter various degrees of difficulty, because of certain uncontrollable factors. Included among some of the methods used for attempting to measure emotional reactivity are as follows:

1. Blood pressure: It rises when one is under some sort of emotional stress.
2. Blood sugar analysis: Under stressful conditions, more sugar enters the blood stream.
3. Pulse rate: Emotional stress causes it to elevate.

4. Galvanic skin response: Similar to the lie detector technique, and measurements are recorded in terms of perspiration on the palms of the hands.

These, as well as others that have been used by investigators of human emotion, have various and perhaps limited degrees of validity. In attempting to assess emotional reactivity, we often encounter the problem of the extent to which we are dealing with a purely physiological response or a purely emotional response. For example, one's pulse rate would be elevated doing some sort of physical exercise. It could likewise be elevated if a person were the object of an embarrassing remark by another. Thus, in this illustration, the elevation of pulse rate could be caused for different reasons, the first being physiological and the second emotional. Then too, the type of emotional pattern is not identified by the measuring device. A joy response and an anger response will likely be the same or nearly the same with regard to rise in pulse rate. These are some of the reasons why it is most difficult to arrive at a high degree of objectivity in studying the emotional aspect of personality.

FACTORS CONCERNED WITH EMOTIONAL STABILITY

Modern society involves a sequence of experiences that are characterized by the necessity for us to adjust. Consequently, it could be said that normal behavior is the result of successful adjustment, and abnormal behavior is the result of unsuccessful adjustment. The degree of adjustment that one achieves depends upon how adequately she is able to satisfy basic needs and fulfill desires within the framework of her environment and the pattern or ways dictated by the society.

As mentioned in the second chapter, stress may be considered as any factor acting internally or externally that renders adaptation difficult, and which induces increased effort on the part of the person to maintain a state of equilibrium within herself and with the environment. When stress is induced as a result of the individual's not being able to meet needs (basic demands) and satisfy desires (wants or wishes), *frustration* or *conflict* results. Frustration occurs when a need is not met, and conflict results when choices must be made between nearly equally attractive alternatives or when basic emotional forces oppose one another. In the emotionally healthy woman, the degree of frustration is ordinarily in proportion to the intensity of the need or desire. That is, she will objectively observe and evaluate the situation to ascertain whether a solution is possible, and if so, what solution best enables her to achieve the fulfillment of needs and desires. However, every person has a *zone of tolerance* or limits for emotional stress within which she normally operates. If the stress becomes considerably greater than the tolerance level, or if the individual has not learned to cope with her problems and objectively and intelligently solve them, some degree of maladjustment can possibly result.

It could be said that the major difference between you, as a so-called normal person, and a criminal confined to prison is that you have the ability to control your emotional impulses to a greater extent than the criminal. Perhaps many of us at one time or another have experienced the same kinds of emotions that have led the abnormal individual to commit violence, but we have been able to hold our powerful and violent emotions in check. This may be an extreme example, but it suggests something of the importance of emotional control in modern society.

An important aspect of controlling the emotions is becoming the ability to function effectively and intelligently in an emotionally charged situation. Success in most life situations hinges on this ability. Extremes of emotional upset must be avoided if the individual is to be able to think and act effectively.

It is sometimes helpful to visualize your emotions as being forces within you that are in a struggle for power with your mind as to which is to control you, your reason, or your emotions. Oftentimes our basic emotions are blind and unconcerned with the welfare of other people, or sometimes, even with our own welfare. Emotional stability has to do with gaining increased mastery over our emotions – not, of course, eliminating them – so that we may behave as intelligent and civilized human beings rather than as savages or children in temper tantrums.

In order to pursue a sensible course in our efforts to acquire desired emotional stability, there are certain factors that need to be considered. They are as follows: (1) characteristics of emotionality, (2) emotional arousals and reactions, and (3) factors that influence emotionality.

CHARACTERISTICS OF EMOTIONALITY

There are Variations in How Long Emotions Last

A child's emotions may last for a few minutes or less and then terminate rather abruptly. The child gets it "out of her system" so to speak by expressing it outwardly. In contrast, some adult emotions may be long and drawn out. As children get older, expressing the emotions by overt action is encumbered by certain social restraints. This is to say that what might be socially acceptable at one age level is not necessarily so at another. This may be a reason why some children develop *moods,* which in a sense are states of emotion drawn out over a period of time and expressed slowly. Typical moods may be that of "sulking" due to restraint or anger, and being "jumpy" from repressed fear. Of course, it is common for these moods to prevail well into adulthood.

There are Differences in the Intensity of Emotions

You will probably recall in your own experience that some persons react rather violently to a situation that to you might appear insignificant. This kind of behavior is likely to reflect one's background and past experience with specific kinds of situations.

Emotions are Subject to Rapid Change

A young child is capable of shifting quickly from laughing to crying, or from anger to joy. Although the reason for this is not definitely known, it may be that there is not as much depth of feeling among children as there is among adults. In addition, it could be due to lack of experience that children have had, as well as their state of intellectual development. We do know that young children have a short attention span, which could cause them to change rapidly from one kind of emotion to another. As we mature into adults rapid change in emotions is likely to wane.

Depending on the Individual, Emotions can appear with Various Degrees of Frequency

As individuals grow and mature, they manage to develop the ability to adjust to situations that previously would have caused an emotional reaction. This is, no doubt, due to the acquisition of more experience with various kinds of emotional situations. As far as children are concerned, they learn what is socially acceptable and what is socially unacceptable through experience. This is particularly true if a child is reprimanded in some way following a violent emotional reaction. For this reason, a child may try to confront situations in ways that do not involve an emotional response. You probably know some adults who tend to react in much the same way.

People Differ in their Emotional Responses

One person when confronted with a situation that instills fear, may run away from the immediate environment (hit and run driver), while another may try to hide. Different reactions of people to emotional situations are probably due to a host of factors. Included among these may be past experiences with a certain kind of emotional situation, willingness of parents and other adults during childhood to help them become more independent, and family relationships in general.

Strength of People's Emotions are Subject to Change

At some age levels certain kinds of emotions may be weak and later become stronger. Conversely, with some young children, emotions that were strong may tend to decline. For example, young children may be timid among strangers, but later when they see there is nothing to fear, the timidity is likely to diminish.

EMOTIONAL AROUSALS AND REACTIONS

If we are to understand the nature of human emotions, we need to take into account some of those factors of emotional arousal and how people might react to them. Many different kinds of emotional patterns have been identified. For purposes here the patterns arbitrarily selected for discussion are fear, worry, anger, jealousy, and joy.

Fear

The term fear from the Old English *fir* may have been derived originally from the German word fahr, meaning danger or peril. In modern times fear is often thought of in terms of anxiety caused by present or impending danger or peril. For example, fear can generally be defined as a more generalized reaction to a vague sense of threat in absence of a specific or realistic dangerous object. However, the terms fear and anxiety are often used loosely and interchangeably. When fearful or anxious, individuals experience unpleasant changes in overt behavior, subjective feelings (including thoughts), and physiological activity.

Fears differ from anxiety in that the former are negative emotional responses to any specific environmental factor. But fears and anxieties are similar in the feelings they arouse; rapid heartbeat, sweating, quivering, heavy breathing, feeling weak or numb in the limbs, dizziness or faintness, muscular tension, the need to eliminate, and a sense of dread – the "fight or flight" response mechanism. Not all people experience all these signs of fear, but most experience some of them.

There are various ways of classifying fears. For purposes of discussion here the two broad classifications of *objective* fears and *irrational* fears will be cited.

Many objective fears are useful and necessary and it is logical that we be afraid of such things as: (1) touching a hot stove, (2) falling from a high place, (3) running into the street without looking for oncoming cars, and (4) having a tooth drilled without anesthesia. These kinds of fears are referred to as *rational* and *adaptive.*

Some fears are said to be *irrational* and *maladaptive.* It is an irrational fear when the objective danger is in disproportion to the amount of distress experienced. These kinds of fears are called *phobias* or *phobic disorders,* among which are (1) fear of high places, (2) fear of closed-in places, (3) fear of receiving injections, (4) fear of working with sharp instruments, (5) fear of the dark, and (6) fear of being alone.

Irrational fears or phobias do not necessarily have to interfere with our lives. It matters little if you are afraid of heights if your lifestyle permits you to avoid high places. However, some irrational fears can be debilitating experiences and interfere greatly with your attempt to lead your daily life. For instance, if one has no tolerance for the sight of blood or being in an environment of medical procedures, one may find her health or life endangered if she refrains from seeking treatment for an injury or disease. In such cases it would clearly be of benefit to do something about such fears.

In another frame of reference it should be mentioned that behavioral explanations of the development and maintenance of fears are based on learning principles. Basically, it is assumed that all behavior, and thus the individual's fear responses, are learned from the environment.

Reporting in Volume 1 of my series on *Stress in Modern Society,* D'Ann Whitehead[1] suggested three paradigms by which learning takes place:

respondent conditioning, operant conditioning, and the two-factor theory of learning.

In *respondent conditioning* if a neutral stimulus is presented simultaneously with the presentation of a fear provoking stimulus, the neutral stimulus will become a conditioned stimulus for fear. Thus on subsequent occasions, the previously neutral stimulus will evoke a fear response. The age-old classic experiment by J.B. Watson and R. Raynor[2] more than eight decades ago illustrates this process. In the experiment, a child, Little Albert, learned to fear a white rat. Initially the child was shown the white rat for which he showed no fear. While the child was paying attention to the rat, he was frightened by a loud sound (striking a steel bar with a hammer held a safe distance behind the child's head). Following several repetitions of this, the child was noticed to be afraid of the rat. The original neutral stimulus (rat), therefore, became a conditioned stimulus to elicit fear. It was later noticed that the child generalized this fear to other "furry" objects, for example, his mother's fur neckpiece. The authors whimsically noted that a dynamically oriented child psychologist examining this child might produce many speculations as to the origin of the fear, but almost certainly would not state in his report that the child was obviously frightened by striking a steel bar behind his head as a white rat was placed in front of him – yet that is how the fear was produced.

Operant conditioning can account for the development of fear or the basis of reinforcement through the environmental contingencies that follow a fear response. For example, the child's fear of the dark may lead to such social reinforcement in terms of parental attention (including bedtime stories, snacks, and the like) at bed time. Similarly, a fear of bugs or dirt may make it "impossible" for the child to help pull weeds in the garden.

The *two-factor theory* was advanced by O.H. Mowrer[3] in the late 1930s and both respondent and operant conditioning are embodied in this concept. According to this theory, fears first developed by respondent conditioning are maintained by operant conditioning. A neutral stimulus is paired with a fear-provoking stimulus and the neutral stimulus becomes a conditioned fear stimulus. If such maneuvers are successful they decrease the level of experienced anxiety or fear. This fear reduction serves to reinforce the behaviors that were instrumental in reducing the fear. For example, if a child is taking a bath and gets water in the nose, the child may develop a fear of baths. In order to reduce the fear and anxiety, she may hide until just before bed time, fall asleep in the living room, or throw a tantrum when told to take a bath. The anxiety reduction experienced by avoiding the bath reinforces continued avoidance of baths.

In my interviews with several female college students the following fears were prominent:

Fear
- of failing in school;
- of letting my parents down;
- of not getting a good job after college;
- of not keeping my health;
- of not having enough money to finish college.

Worry

This might be an imaginary form of fear, and it can be a fear not aroused directly from one's environment. Worry can be aroused by imagining a situation that could possibly arise: that is, one could worry about other family members. Since worries are likely to be caused by *imaginary* rather than *real* conditions, they are not likely to be found in abundance in very young children. Perhaps the reason for this is that they have not reached a stage of intellectual development where they might imagine certain things that could cause worry. Among some adults worry is a constant problem, and many will find things to worry about. Controlling worry is a difficult problem for those adults who have problems in adjusting. In my surveys of various populations of women the following were among the most prominent worries:

Worry
- about my family;
- about my parents getting old;
- about my financial position;
- about not being a success;
- about where the country is headed.

Anger

This emotional response tends to occur more frequently than fear. This is probably due to the fact that there are more conditions that incite anger. In the case of children, they quickly learn that anger may get attention that otherwise would not be forthcoming (can you think of any "spoiled" adults who react in this manner?). It is likely that as children get older they may show more anger responses than fear responses because they soon see that there is not as much to fear as they originally thought.

Because of individual differences in people, there is a wide variation in anger responses, and as mentioned previously, these responses are either impulsive or inhibited. It should be recalled that in impulsive responses, one manifests an overt action against another person or an object, such as kicking a door. This form of child behavior is also sometimes manifested by some "adults."

In discussing anger, the condition of *aggression* should also be taken into account. Aggression literally means, "to attack." This ordinarily is provoked by anger and can result in hostile action. Thus, anger is the emotional pattern and it is outwardly demonstrated by aggression. It is important to point out the difference between aggressive behavior and *assertive* behavior. The latter form of behavior has received a great deal of attention in recent years, and rightly so. Self-assertiveness should be considered a basic role in one's life. All of us have a need for self-reliance and confidence in our abilities. This need can be met by asserting ourselves in a manner through which we pursue our personal goals without too much dependence on others. Certainly one can be assertive without being aggressive.

My studies of women reveal that the following things seem to cause the most anger:

1. People who don't know how to drive.
2. People who think they are better than I am.
3. People who try to tell me what to do.
4. People who are always complaining.
5. Having to wait too long in line for almost everything.

Jealousy

This response usually occurs when one feels a threat of loss of affection. Many psychologists believe that jealousy is closely related to anger. Because of this, a person may build up resentment against another person. Jealousy can be very devastating and every effort should be made to avoid it.

Jealousy is concerned with social interactions that involve persons one likes. There are various ways in which the individual may respond. These include: (1) being aggressive toward the one of whom she is jealous, (2) withdrawing from the person whose affections she thinks have been lost, and (3) possible development of an "I don't care" attitude.

In some cases, individuals will not respond in any of the above ways. They might try to excel over the person of whom they are jealous. In other words, they might tend to do things to impress the person whose affections they think have been lost.

Joy

This pleasant emotion is one that we strive for because it is so important in maintaining emotional stability. Causes of joy differ from one age level to another, and from one person to another at the same age level. This is to say that what might be a joyful situation for one person might not necessarily be so for another.

Joy is expressed in various ways, but the most common are laughing and smiling, the latter being a restrained form of laughter. Some people respond to joy with a state of body relaxation. This is difficult to detect because it has little or no overt manifestation. However, it may be noticed when one compares it with body tension caused by unpleasant emotions.

It seems appropriate to close this discussion about emotional arousals and reactions with some comments about *crying*. This is particularly important because as was mentioned in Chapter 3, traditionally women have been expected to express their emotions while men are expected to suppress them. In fact, it used to be believed that it was "sissy to cry," and this pertained essentially to males.

Crying can be a response to a pleasant emotion as well as an unpleasant one. "She laughed until she cried" and "I was so mad I cried."

The study of crying has become an important area of research and a review of the literature on the subject can be summarized as follows:

- Crying is now placed solidly within the context of children's normal development.
- All people cry from five to 10 ounces of *basal* tears each day (the eye's constant and ordinary source of lubrication).
- Women cry, on average, from four to five times more than men.
- It is perfectly normal for boys and men to cry.

Finally, one source[4] indicates that there is an old Chinese proverb that states, "Children must cry to grow."

GUIDELINES FOR THE DEVELOPMENT
OF EMOTIONAL STABILITY

It is important to set forth some guidelines if we are to meet with any degree of success in our attempts to provide for emotional stability. The reason for this is to assure, at least to some extent, that our efforts at attaining optimum emotional stability will be based somewhat on a scientific approach. These guidelines might well take the form of *valid concepts of emotional stability*. The following list of concepts is submitted with this general idea in mind.

1. *An emotional response may be brought about by a goal's being furthered or thwarted.* Serious attempts should be made by those responsible to assure a successful experience in a given environment such as home, school, or job. In the school setting, this can be accomplished in part by attempting to provide for individual differences within given school experiences. The school, home, or job setting should be such that each person derives a feeling of personal worth through making some sort of positive contribution.

2. *Self-realization experiences should be constructive.* The opportunity for creative experiences that afford the individual a chance for self-realization should be inherent in the home, school, or on the job. Individuals should plan with others to see that specific environmental activities are meeting their needs, and as a result, involve constructive experiences.

3. *In the case of children, as they develop, emotional reactions tend to become less violent and more discriminating.* A well-planned program of school experiences and wholesome home activities should be such that they provide for release of aggression in a socially acceptable manner.

4. *Emotional reactions tend to increase beyond normal expectancy toward the constructive or destructive on the balance of furthering or hindering experiences of the individual.* For some persons the confidence they need in order to be able to face the problems of life

may come through physical expression. Therefore, such experiences as pleasurable physical activity in the form of recreation in the away-from-work situation have tremendous potential to help contribute toward a solid base for emotional stability.

5. *Depending on certain factors, one's own feelings may be accepted or rejected by the individual.* All environmental experiences should make people feel good and have confidence in themselves. Satisfactory self-concept is closely related to body control; physical activity oriented experiences might be considered as one of the best ways of contributing to it.

OPPORTUNITIES FOR THE DEVELOPMENT OF EMOTIONAL STABILITY IN VARIOUS KINDS OF ENVIRONMENTS

Environments, such as the school, home, and worksite, have the potential to provide for emotional stability. The extent to which this actually occurs is dependent primarily upon the kind of emotional climate provided by individuals responsible for it, such as teachers, parents, employers, and others. For this reason, it appears pertinent to examine some of the potential opportunities that exist for the development of emotional stability in these environments. The following descriptive list is submitted for this purpose.

1. *Release of aggression in a socially acceptable manner.* This appears to be an outstanding way in which sports and recreational experiences help provide women with opportunities to improve upon emotional stability. For example, hitting a tennis ball can afford a socially acceptable way of releasing aggression.

2. *Inhibition of direct response to unpleasant emotions.* This does not necessarily mean that feelings concerned with such unpleasant emotions as fear and anger should be completely restrained. On the contrary, the interpretation should be that such feelings can take place less frequently in a wholesome school, home or work environment. This means that opportunities should be provided to relieve tension rather than aggravate it.

3. *Promotion of pleasant emotions.* Perhaps there is too much concern with suppressing unpleasant emotions and not enough attention given to promotion of pleasant ones. This means that life experiences should provide a range of activities where all can succeed. Thus, all women should be afforded the opportunity for success at least most of the time.

4. *Understanding about the ability and achievement of others.* In life experiences emphasis can be placed upon achievement of the group. Team play and group effort is important in most situations, whether it be in school, or on the job.

5. *Being able to make a mistake without being ostracized.* In the various environments someone should serve as a catalyst who helps each individual understand the idea of trial and error. Emphasis can be placed on *trying* and that one can learn not only from her own mistakes but from the mistakes of others as well.

EVALUATING INFLUENCES OF THE ENVIRONMENT ON THE DEVELOPMENT OF EMOTIONAL STABILITY

What we are essentially concerned with here is how an individual can make some sort of valid evaluation of the extent to which a particular environment contributes to emotional stability. This means that some attempt should be made to assess an environment with reference to whether or not these experiences are providing for emotional stability.

One such approach would be to refer back to the list of "opportunities for the development of emotional stability in various kinds of environments" suggested in the immediately preceding discussion. These opportunities have been converted into a rating scale as follows:

1. The environmental experience provides for release of aggression in a socially acceptable manner.
   4. most of the time
   3. some of the time
   2. occasionally
   1. infrequently

2. The environmental experience provides for inhibition of direct response of unpleasant emotions.
    4. most of the time
    3. some of the time
    2. occasionally
    1. infrequently

3. The environmental experience provides for promotion of pleasant emotions.
    4. most of the time
    3. some of the time
    2. occasionally
    1. infrequently

4. The environmental experience provides for an understanding about the ability and achievements of others.
    4. most of the time
    3. some of the time
    2. occasionally
    1. infrequently

5. The environmental experience provides for being able to make a mistake without being ostracized.
    4. most of the time
    3. some of the time
    2. occasionally
    1. infrequently

If one makes these ratings objectively and conscientiously, a reasonably good procedure for evaluation is provided. Ratings can be made periodically to see if positive changes appear to be taking place. Ratings can be made for a single experience, a group of experiences, or for the total environmental experience. This procedure can help one identify the extent to which environmental experiences and/or conditions under which the experiences take place are contributing to emotional stability.

THE EMOTIONALLY HEALTHY PERSON

It seems appropriate to close this chapter by mentioning some of the characteristics of emotionally healthy persons. As we look at some of these characteristics we must recognize that they are not absolute or static. We are not always happy, and we sometimes find ourselves in situations where we are not overly confident. In fact, sometimes we may feel downright inadequate to solve commonplace problems that occur in our daily lives.

1. Emotionally healthy persons have achieved basic harmony within themselves and a workable relationship with others. They are able to function effectively, and usually happily, even though they are well aware of the limitations and rigors involved in human existence.

2. Emotionally healthy persons manage to adapt to the demands of environmental conditions with emotional responses that are appropriate in degree and kind to the stimuli and situations that generally fall within the range of what is considered "normal" in various environments.

3. Emotionally healthy persons face problems directly and seek realistic and plausible solutions to them. They try to free themselves from excessive and unreal anxieties, worries and fears, even though they are aware that there is much to be concerned with and much to be anxious about in our complex modern society.

4. Emotionally healthy persons have developed a guiding philosophy of life and have a set of values that are acceptable to themselves and that are generally in harmony with those values of society that are reasonable and conducive to human happiness.

5. Emotionally healthy persons accept themselves and are willing to deal with the world as it exists in reality. They accept what cannot be changed at a particular time and place and they build and derive satisfaction within the framework of their own potentialities and those of their environment.

6. Emotionally healthy persons tend to be happy, and they tend to have enthusiasm for living. They do not focus their attention

exclusively upon what they consider to be their inadequacies, weaknesses, and "bad" qualities. They view those around them in this way too.

7. Emotionally healthy persons have a variety of satisfying interests and they maintain a balance between their work, routine responsibilities, and recreation. They find constructive and satisfying outlets for creative expression in the interests that they undertake.

This list of characteristics of emotionally healthy persons presents a near-ideal situation and obviously none of us operate at such high levels at all times. However, they might well be considered as suitable guidelines for which we might strive in helping us deal with and possibly prevent unpleasant emotional stress.

Chapter 6

WOMEN'S HEALTH AND STRESS

There appear to be two general factors to consider with regard to stress and health. First, objective evidence continues to accumulate to support the idea that prolonged stressful conditions can be most detrimental to the health of some individuals. The second factor is that, along with new and modern techniques of relieving stress, there are many traditional health practices that have long helped people gain better control of their lives and thus reduce the negative effects of stressful living. It is the primary function here to deal with the second factor in the hope that the discussion will have a positive impact upon eliminating, or at least minimizing the conditions concerned with the first factor. To this end, discussions in this chapter will deal with what I will call the *health triad:* (1) nutrition and diet, (2) physical activity and exercise, and (3) body restoration.

NUTRITION AND DIET

The 18th century gastronomist Anthelme Brillat-Savarin, famous for his book, *The Physiology of Taste,* once proclaimed "Tell me what you eat and I will tell you what you are." The more modern adage "You are what you eat" could well have been derived from this old quotation. And, of course, it is true.

At one time eating was fun and enjoyable until recent years when many of us have become victims of the "don't eat this, don't eat that" syndrome. The fact is that because certain aspects of nutrition and diet have become so controversial, many people in the general public have become more or less confused about the entire matter. Therefore, it is the purpose of this section of the chapter to attempt to clear up at least some of this confusion, as well as to consider nutrition and diet as they are concerned with stress.

At the outset it is stated forcefully and unequivocally that any consideration of one's nutritional problems, eating habits, dietary concerns and the like should be undertaken in consultation with, or under the supervision of a physician and/or a qualified nutritionist.

Nutrition

Nutrition can be described as the sum of the processes by which a person takes in and utilizes food substances; that is, the nourishment of the body by food. These processes consist of (1) ingestion, (2) digestion, (3) absorption, and (4) assimilation.

Ingestion is derived from the Latin word *ingestus,* meaning "to take in," and in this context it means taking in food, or the act of eating. The process of digestion, involves the breaking down or conversion of food into substances that can be *absorbed* through the lining of the intestinal tract and into the blood and used by the body. *Assimilation* is concerned with the incorporation or conversion of nutrients into *protoplasm,* which is the essential material making up living cells.

The body needs many nutrients or foods to keep it functioning properly. These nutrients fall into the broad groups of proteins, carbohydrates, fats, vitamins, and minerals. (Although water is not a nutrient in the strictest sense of the word it must be included, because nutrition cannot take place without it.)

Three major functions of nutrients are (1) building and repair of all body tissues, (2) regulation of all body functions, and (3) providing fuel for the body's energy needs. Although all of the nutrients can do their best work when they are in combination with other nutrients, each still has its own vital role to play.

Digestion

Any discussion of nutrition should take the subject of digestion into account. The digestive system is more than 30 feet long from beginning to end, and the chemical processes that occur within the walls of the mucus-lined hollow tube are somewhat complex in nature. From the moment that food is taken into the mouth until waste products are excreted, the body's chemical laboratory is at work. The principal parts of this system are the alimentary canal, consisting of the oral cavity, pharynx, esophagus, stomach, small intestine, and large intestine. Two additional organs are necessary to complete the digestive system. These are the liver and the pancreas, which both connect to the small intestine. It is from these two organs that many of the essentially digestive juices are secreted.

As mentioned previously, the function of the digestive system is to change the composition of food we ingest. Reduced to simpler chemical substances, the foods can be readily absorbed through the lining of the intestines for distribution by the circulatory system to the millions of body cells. These end products of digestion are in the form of simple sugars, fatty acids, amino acids, minerals, and vitamins.

Digestion is also accomplished by mechanical action. First, the food is broken down by the grinding action of the teeth. This tremendously increases the food surface area upon which the various digestive juices can act. It is then swallowed and eventually moved through the alimentary canal by the process of *peristalsis*. This is a series of muscular contractions which mix the contents of the digestive tract and keep it on the move.

Some people have trouble digesting milk because of what is called lactose intolerance. This means that the enzyme lactate may be decreasing, and this enzyme is needed to break down lactose, a form of sugar found in milk. One may wish to use a substitute for regular milk such as buttermilk, yogurt, or cheese. Also there is a product call lactaid, which is a reduced lactose milk.

Digestion and Stress

Many of the women in my studies reported digestive disturbance when they are under stress. This is commonly known as *nervous indigestion*. In this regard, the digestive tract is exceedingly responsive to one's emotional state. Food eaten under happy conditions tends to be readily digested. On the contrary, digestion may be impeded and even stopped for a considerable period of time (as much as a day or more) if severe emotional stress occurs. Extensive nervous connections in the digestive tract tend to make its organs especially susceptible to disorders caused by stress. Examples of some of these disorders are nausea, diarrhea, and colitis (inflammation of the large bowel). In such disorders the organs involved may not necessarily be diseased and there may only be an impaired functioning of the organ. However, many authorities agree that prolonged emotional stress can lead to serious diseases of the digestive tract. Two of my collaborators on a stress project, Donald Morse and Robert Pollack[1] contend that stress is the principal reason for digestive disturbances. For example, in their work on stress and saliva it was found that stress causes dry mouth. This is particularly important because digestion starts in the mouth and saliva is needed to start the digestion of starch.

Diet

The term *diet* is an all inclusive one used to refer to foods and liquids regularly consumed. The question often raised is: What constitutes a balanced diet? A balanced diet means, essentially, that along with sufficient fluids, one should include foods from the four basic food groups. These are the dairy group, meat group, vegetable and fruit group, and bread and cereal group.

A guide to a balanced diet was prepared by the staff of the United States Senate Select Committee on Nutrition and Human Needs. This committee spent a great deal of time on hearings and research, and some of its recommendations are listed as follows:

1. Eat less meat and more fish and poultry.
2. Replace whole milk with skim milk.
3. Reduce intake of eggs, butter and other high-cholesterol sources.
4. Cut back on sugars to 15 percent of daily caloric intake.
5. Reduce intake of salt to a total of three grams per day.
6. Eat more fruit, vegetables, and whole grain.

These recommendations are directed to the general population. However, one important fact is good to keep in mind, and this is that eating is an individual matter. The problem may not be so much one of following an arbitrary diet, but perhaps is more related to knowing what foods and proportions of foods one functions best on.

It was mentioned previously that you are what you eat. This old adage has been brought more clearly into focus because researchers now know that our bodies synthesize food substances known as *neurotransmitters.* Prominent nutritionists tend to be of the opinion that these neurotransmitters relay messages to the brain that in turn affect our moods, sex drive, appetite, and even personality. This is to say that adding a certain food or omitting another could be just what a person might need. It is believed that when a person is stressed the body becomes less able to make use of protein. Therefore, the general recommendation is that after any kind of stress one should eat more meat, fish or milk products. Also because stress depletes the supply of vitamin C and potassium, these can be replaced by eating extra portions of citrus products.

The diets of some families include too much of certain foods that can be potentially harmful. A case in point is the intake of *cholesterol*. Excessive amounts of this chemical component of animal oils and fats are deposited in the blood vessels and may be a factor in the causation of hardening of the arteries leading to a heart attack.

Cholesterol has become one of the health buzzwords in recent years. The importance of cholesterol as a risk factor prompted the first National Cholesterol Conference, held November 9 to 11, 1988. This meeting was sponsored by the National Cholesterol Education Program Coordinating Committee, which included some 25 member organizations. This conference was a somewhat unique forum in that researchers, physicians, and policy and program experts shared new knowledge and program successes in the rapidly changing field of cholesterol.

The universal interest in this risk factor is certainly justified by such estimates as:

1. More than 50 percent of Americans have a cholesterol level that is too high.
2. Only about eight percent of Americans know their cholesterol level.
3. As many as 250,000 lives could be saved each year if citizens were tested and took action to reduce their cholesterol.
4. For every one percent you lower your cholesterol, you reduce your risk of heart attack by two percent.
5. If your cholesterol level is 265 or over, you have four times the risk of a heart attack as someone with 190 or less.
6. Nine out of ten people can substantially reduce their cholesterol level by diet.

Physicians vary widely in their beliefs about safe levels of cholesterol and a few years ago a broad range of 150 to 300 was considered normal. However, thoughts on this matter have changed radically. For example, the National Heart, Lung and Blood Institute has announced more stringent guidelines. It is now believed that total blood cholesterol should not go over 200 (this means 200 milligrams of total cholesterol per deciliter of blood).

It should be mentioned that not all cholesterol is bad. Actually, there are two kinds of lipoproteins, low-density lipoproteins (LDL) and high-density (HDL). The former is considered "bad" because the cholesterol it carries in the blood is associated with an increased risk of atherosclerosis (hardening of the inner lining of the arteries). HDL (good) appears to clear excess cholesterol from the arteries while LDL (bad) can lead to cholesterol buildup in the artery walls. (There are also certain approved drugs that a physician can recommend to lower abnormally high cholesterol levels.)

It is not absolutely necessary to have a balanced diet every day. The body is capable of compensating for an imbalance in the nutrients one fails to get if the shortage is made up within a reasonable period of time. In other words, it is not necessary to have an exactly balanced diet at every meal. Indeed, it is possible to miss meals – even go for several days without food – and show little or no signs of malnutrition. The important consideration seems to be the quality of total intake over periods of time.

Diet and Stress

Most writers on the subject of stress emphasize the importance of diet as a general health measure. However, the following question arises: Are there any specific forms of diet that can contribute to the prevention of stress and/or help us cope with it? In this regard, J. Daniel Palm[2] once developed the theory that many stress-initiated disorders are related to problems that originate in the regulation of the blood sugar level. This theory, developed as an extension of the data derived from controlled research, states that an insufficiency of sugar in the blood supplied to the brain is a detrimental condition, and therefore a stress as it initiates physiological responses and behavioral changes that develop into a variety of disorders. A deficiency of blood sugar, which is known to be associated with a variety of disorders, is seen not as a consequence of the disease but a primary and original physiological stress. Behavioral changes may be inadequate or inappropriate attempts of the stress-affected persons to compensate. It is believed that if the stress of an insufficiency of blood sugar can be prevented, various kinds of abnormal behavior can be controlled. To eliminate this stress of deficiency of blood sugar, a dietary program was proposed. This diet was based on the metabolic characteristics of *fructose* (fruit sugar) and its advantageous use when exchanged for glucose or other carbohydrates, which are digested to glucose and then absorbed (fructose itself is a normal constituent of sucrose, which is ordinary table sugar; it also occurs naturally in many fruits and constitutes half the content of honey).

With regard to the above, the previously-mentioned Donald Morse and Robert Pollack caution that an excess of fructose can also be a problem. This occurs more from the ingestion of soft drinks and processed foods where the concentration of fructose is often higher than it is in fruits and juices. It has also been found that when fructose intake is raised to about 20 percent of a person's daily diet (up from the average of 10-12 percent), total cholesterol may increase more than 11 percent and triglycerides are elevated slightly above 56 percent.

For some time a great deal of controversy has emerged as a result of what has been called *megavitamin therapy*. This concerns the use of certain vitamins in massive doses – sometimes as much as 1,000 times the U.S. Daily Reference Intake. The proponents for megavitamin therapy believe that massive doses of such vitamins, particularly vitamin C and in some cases the B complex vitamins, will prevent certain diseases and very significantly extend life. On the contrary, opponents of the practice maintain that it is not only useless, but in some instances, harmful as well.

There is support in some quarters for massive dosages of certain vitamins as an important factor in surviving stress. In fact, there is a classification of vitamins sold over the counter that are called *stress formula vitamins,* and they go by a variety of brand names. The formula for these is one that includes large amounts of vitamin C and vitamin B complex. (Anyone contemplating utilizing a vitamin supplement over and about the U.S. Daily Reference Intake should do so in consultation with a physician and/or a qualified nutritionist.

It is certainly interesting that one of the most popular claims for nutritional supplements is that they can effectively eliminate or reduce stress. Several years ago governmental regulatory agencies cautioned vitamin manufacturers that implied this on their labels. However, as mentioned, the word stress still appears on some products, and the Food and Drug Administration has been petitioned to ban vitamins and "stress formulas," because there was no proof that their ingredients were beneficial in this regard. Most claim protection against the effects of daily stress, or overwork, and usually contain large amounts of vitamins, as well as minerals, or herbal products. Although generally not harmful, some formulations have enough vitamin C to cause diarrhea, and dosages of vitamin B6 that can produce nerve damage if taken over long periods of time.[3]

Practically all theories have enthusiastic proponents as well as equally enthusiastic opponents, and this sometimes results in a great deal of confusion among all of us. The fact that the human organism is so complicated and complex makes any kind of research connected with it extremely difficult. Nevertheless, scholars in the scientific community continue to make important inquiries into the study of human needs. It is emphasized again, and forcefully, that individuals concerned in any way with their own specific dietary problems should consult a physician and/or a qualified nutritionist for guidance.

Physical Activity and Exercise

When used in connection with the human organism, the term physical means a concern for the body and its needs. The term *activity* derives from the word "active," one meaning of which is the requirement of action. Thus, when the two words physical and activity are used together, it implies body action. This is a broad term and could include any voluntary and/or involuntary body movement. When such body movement is practiced for the purpose of developing and maintaining *physical fitness,* it is ordinarily referred to as *physical exercise.* This section of the chapter is concerned with both the broad area of physical activity and the more specific area of physical exercise, and will take into account how these factors are concerned with all around health as well as how they relate to stress.

The Physical Aspect of Personality

One point of departure in discussing the physical aspect of personality could be to state that "everybody has a body." Some are short, some are tall, some are lean, and some are fat. People come in different sizes, but all of them have a certain innate capacity that is influenced by the environment.

As far as human beings are concerned – from early childhood through adulthood – it might be said that the body is our base of operation, what could be called our "physical base." The other components of the total personality – social, emotional, and intellectual – are somewhat vague. Although these are manifested in various ways, we do not actually see them as we do the physical aspect. Consequently, it becomes all important even as children, that a serious attempt be made to gain control over the physical aspect, or what is known as basic body control. The ability to do this will vary from one person to another. It will depend to a large extent upon our status of physical fitness.

The broad area of physical fitness can be broken down into certain components, and it is important that individuals achieve to the best of their natural ability as far as these components are concerned. There is not complete agreement as far as identification of the components of physical fitness are concerned. However, the following information provided by the President's Council of Physical Fitness and Sports considers certain components as basic:

Muscular Strength

This refers to the contraction power of muscles. The strength of muscles is usually measured with dynamometers or tensiometers, which record the amount of force particular muscle groups can apply in a single maximum effort. Our existence and effectiveness depend upon our muscles. All movements of the body or any of its parts are impossible without action by muscles attached to the skeleton. Muscles perform vital functions of the body as well. The heart is a muscle; death occurs when it ceases to contract. Breathing, digestion, and elimination are dependent upon muscular contractions. These vital muscular functions are influenced by exercising the skeletal muscles; the heart beats faster; the blood circulates through the body at a greater rate, breathing becomes deep and rapid, and perspiration breaks out on the surface of the skin.

Muscular Endurance

Muscular endurance is the ability of muscles to perform work. Two variations of muscular endurance are recognized: *isometric,* whereby a maximum static muscular contraction is held and *isotonic* whereby the muscles continue to raise and lower a submaximal load as in weight training or performing push-ups. In the isometric form, the muscles maintain a fixed length; in the isotonic form, they alternatively shorten and lengthen. Muscular endurance must assume some muscular strength. However, there are distinctions between the two; muscle groups of the same strength may possess different degrees of endurance.

Circulatory-Respiratory Endurance

Circulatory respiratory endurance is characterized by moderate contractions of large muscle groups for relatively long periods of time, during which maximal adjustments of the circulatory-respiratory system to the activity are necessary, as in distance running and swimming. Obviously, strong and enduring muscles are needed. However, by themselves they are not enough; they do not guarantee well-developed circulatory-respiratory functions.

As far as the physical aspect of personality is concerned one of our major objectives should be directed to maintaining a suitable level of physical fitness, which will be one of the topics of the ensuing discussion.

Maintain a Suitable Level of Physical Fitness

Physical fitness presupposes an adequate intake of good food and an adequate amount of rest and sleep, but beyond these things, activity involving all the big muscles of the body is essential. Just how high a level of physical fitness should be maintained from one stage of life to another is difficult to answer because we must raise the following question: Fitness for what? Obviously, the young varsity female athlete needs to think of a level of fitness far above that which will concern the average middle-aged woman.

Physical fitness has been described in different ways by different people; however, when all of these descriptions are put together it is likely that they will be characterized more by their similarities than their differences. For purposes here, physical fitness will be thought of as the level of ability of the human organism to perform certain tasks or, put another way, the fitness to perform various specified tasks requiring muscular effort.

A reasonable question to raise at this point is: Why is a reasonably high level of physical fitness desirable in modern times when there are so many effort-saving devices available that, for many people, strenuous activity is really not necessary anymore? One possible answer to this is that all of us stand at the end of a long line of ancestors, all of whom lived at least long enough to have children because they were fit and vigorous, strong enough to survive in the face of savage beasts and savage men, and able to work hard. Only the fit survived. As a matter of fact, not very far back in your family tree, you can find people who had to be rugged and extremely active in order to live. Vigorous action and physical ruggedness are our biological heritage. Possibly because of the kind of background that we have, our bodies simply function better when we are active.

Most child development specialists agree that vigorous play in childhood is essential for the satisfactory growth of the various organs and systems of the body. It has been said that "play is the business of childhood." To conduct this "business" successfully and happily, the child should be physically fit. Good nutrition, rest, and properly conducted physical activities in school can do much to develop and maintain the physical fitness of children and youth. Continuing this practice throughout life should be an essential goal for all of us.

The word *exercise* may tend to have strong moralistic overtones. Like so many things that are said to be "good for you," it also tends to give rise to certain feelings of boredom and resentment. Thus, many people draw more than facetious pleasure in repeating the old sayings: "When I feel like exercising, I lie down quickly until the feeling goes away," and "I get my exercise serving as pall-bearer for my friends who exercised."

As an "old gym teacher," I can summarize my feelings about exercising and maintaining some level of physical fitness by saying that doing so makes possible types of meaningful experiences in life that are not otherwise available to you. These experiences include all manner of physical activity and exercise, including indoor and outdoor sports; and they also include the rich and satisfying interpersonal relationships that are usually associated with these activities. But maintaining some level of physical fitness has still another value that is usually not fully appreciated. This value has to do with the idea that the entire personality of every individual rests upon, and is dependent upon, its physical base. The entire personality – which is to say, all of the social, emotional, and intellectual components – is threatened when the physical component, the base of operation is weak and unreliable. It has been claimed by fitness enthusiasts that academic performance, emotional control, and social adjustments are improved if an adequate level of physical fitness is improved and many case histories and clinical data would tend to support this contention. However, at the moment, it could be argued that a reasonably solid physical base is more likely than a shaky one to serve you as a successful launching pad for other personality resources. In other words, you will likely do better in everything you undertake if you feel good, your vitality is high, and you are capable of prolonged effort.

Types of Exercises

Generally speaking, there are three types of exercises: (1) *proprioceptive-facilitative,* (2) *isotonic,* and (3) *isometric.* (In reading this section of the chapter the reader is asked to refer back to the discussion of the components of physical fitness – muscular strength, muscular endurance, and circulatory-respiratory endurance.)

Proprioceptive-Facilitative Exercises

These exercises are those that consist of various refined patterns of movement. Important in the performance of these exercises are these factors involved in movement: (1) time, (2) force, (3) space, and (4) flow.

Time is concerned with how long it takes to complete a movement. For example, a movement can be slow and deliberate, such as a child trying to create a body movement to depict a falling snowflake. On the other hand, a movement might be made with sudden quickness, such as starting to run for a goal on a signal.

Force needs to be applied to set the body or one of its segments in motion and to change its speed and/or direction. Thus, force is concerned with how much strength is required for movement. Swinging the arms requires less strength than attempting to propel the body over the surface area with a standing long jump.

In general, there are two factors concerned with *space*. These are the amount of space required to perform a particular movement and the utilization of available space.

All movements involve some degree of rhythm in their performance. Thus, *flow* is the sequence of movement involving rhythmic motion.

The above factors are included in all body movements in various degrees. The degree to which each is used effectively in combination will determine the extent to which the movement is performed with skill. This is a basic essential in the performance of proprioceptive-facilitative exercises. In addition, various combinations of the following are involved in the performance of this type of exercise.

1. *Muscular power*. Ability to release maximum muscular force in the shortest time. Example: Standing long jump.
2. *Agility*. Speed in changing body position or in changing direction. Example: Dodging run.
3. *Speed*. Rapidity with which successive movements of the same kind are performed. Example: Short running dash, such as required in the game of tennis.
4. *Flexibility*. Range of movement in a joint or sequence of joints. Example: Any activity that requires bending at one or more joints.
5. *Balance*. Ability to maintain position and equilibrium both in movement (dynamic balance) and while stationary (static balance). Examples: Walking on a line or balance beam (dynamic); standing on one foot (static).
6. *Coordination*. Working together of muscles and organs of the body in the performance of a specific task. Example: Throwing or catching an object.

Isotonic Exercises

These are types of exercises with which most people are familiar. An isotonic exercise involves the amount of resistance one can overcome during one application of force through the full range of motion in a given joint or joints. An example of this would be picking up a weight and flexing the elbows while lifting the weight to shoulder height.

Isometric Exercises

Although isometrics do not provide much in the way of improvement of normal range of motion and endurance, they are most useful in increasing the strength and volume of muscles. In isometrics the muscle is contracted, but the length of the muscle is generally the same during contraction as during relaxation. The contraction is accomplished by keeping two joints rigid while at the same time contracting the muscles(s) between the joints. A maximal amount of force is applied against a fixed resistance during one all-out effort. An example of this is pushing or pulling against an immovable object. Let us say if you place your hands against a wall and push with as much force as you can, you have effected the contraction of certain muscles while their length has remained essentially the same.

Importance of Physical Exercise in Reducing Stress

Exercise can provide a variety of stress reduction benefits for many individuals. Many people under stress experience a "fight or flight" response characterized by increased muscle tension, blood pressure, and heart rate due to the release of stress-related hormones and increased sympathetic nervous system activities. These are designed to increase alertness and improve strength for fight, or greater speed for flight. However, if this state persists, or is not followed by a period of relaxation, a variety of physical and emotional problems can ensue. Exercise may relieve stress by providing an outlet for increased energy stores that have not been utilized. In some instances, exercise can provide emotional benefits, as stressful thoughts are replaced by focusing on the activity being pursued. There may also be increased endorphin secretion, which promotes a sense of well-being or euphoria, and greater resistance to pain. We often hear of the "runner's high" and people feeling good about themselves after exercising. When we stop exercising, heart rate and blood pressure fall, breathing becomes slower and more regular, and muscle tension is dissipated. In addition, during the post-exercise period, we are apt to fall into a relaxed and contemplative state that provides other emotional benefits.

Physical Activities for Stressful Situations

Many occupations and professions produce various kinds of stressful conditions, and many of these occur in the immediate work environment. The foregoing discussion focused on the importance of physical activity in helping one deal with stress. The present discussion is concerned with a person's active behavior in a stressful situation. More specifically, what can one (executive, office worker, teacher, and others) do in the way of physical activity to deal with a stressful situation in the immediate environment?

What then are some of the physical activities that one can engage in as a reaction to a stressful situation? Obviously, it would not be appropriate to engage in isotonics by dropping to the floor to do pushups or to break into a jog around the room. Isometrics are recommended for this purpose and they can be performed in a more or less subtle manner and not necessarily be noticed by others. The following are some possibilities, and certainly creative individuals will be able to think of others.

Hand and Head Press
Interweave fingers and place hands at the back of the head with elbows pointing out. Push the head forward with the hands. Although this can be done while standing, it can also be done while sitting at a desk or table and is less conspicuous.

Wall Press
Stand with the back against the wall. Allow the arms to hang down at the sides. Turn hands toward the wall and press the wall with the palms, keeping the arms straight (a useful activity when the boss has your "back to the wall").

Hand Pull
Bend the right elbow and bring the right hand in with the palms up close to the front of the body. Put the left hand in the right hand. Try to curl the right arm upward while simultaneously resisting with the left hand. Repeat, using the opposite pressure. This can be done while standing or sitting at a desk or table.

Hand Push
The hands are clasped with the palms together close to the chest with the elbows pointing out. Press the hands together firmly.

Leg Press

While sitting at a desk or table, cross the left ankle over the right ankle. The feet are on the floor and the legs are at about a right angle. Try to straighten the right leg while resisting with the left leg. Repeat with the right ankle over the left ankle.

The Gripper

Place one hand in the other and grip hard. Another variation is to grip an object. While standing, this could be the back of a chair or, while sitting, it could be the arms of a chair or the seat.

Chair Push

While sitting at a desk or table with the hands on the armrests of the chair, push down hard with the hands. The entire buttocks can be raised from the chair seat. One or both feet can be lifted off the floor, or both can remain in contact with the floor.

Hip Lifter

While sitting at a desk or table, lift one buttock after the other from the chair seat. Try to keep the head from moving. The hands can be placed at the sides of the chair seat for balance.

Heel and Toe

From a standing position, rise on the toes. Come back down on the heels while raising both the toes and the balls of the feet.

Fist Clencher

Clench fists and then open the hands extending the fingers as far as possible.

This short list is comprised of representative examples of isometric exercises, and can actually be referred to as stress exercises. These types of activities can be performed easily in most environments. Wherever they are performed it might be well to observe the following suggestions. For each contraction, maintain tension for no more than eight seconds (or even less). Do little breathing during the contraction; breathe deeply between contractions.

The isometric exercises recommended here have met with success with persons who have practiced them in any environment. (Chapter 10 will go into detail on deep muscle relaxation to reduce stress.)

BODY RESTORATION

To be effective on the job and in other pursuits and to enjoy leisure to the utmost, periodic recuperation is an essential ingredient in daily living patterns. Body restoration in the form of rest and sleep provide us with the means of revitalizing ourselves to meet the challenges of our responsibilities. It is no wonder that an old Chinese proverb states that: *Sleep is a priceless treasure and the more one has the better it is.*

Fatigue

Any consideration given to body restoration should perhaps begin with a discussion of fatigue. In order to keep fatigue at a minimum and in its proper proportion in the cycle of everyday activities, nature has provided us with ways to help combat and reduce it. First, however, we should consider what fatigue is so that it may then be easier to cope with it.

There are two types of fatigue, *acute* and *chronic*. Acute fatigue is a natural outcome of sustained exertion. It is due to such physical factors as the accumulation of byproducts of muscular exertion in the blood and excessive "oxygen debt" – the inability of the body to take in as much oxygen as is being consumed by muscular work. Psychological considerations may also be important in acute fatigue. An individual who becomes bored with what she is doing and who becomes preoccupied with the discomfort involved will become fatigued much sooner than if she is highly motivated to do the same thing, is not bored, and does not think about the discomfort.

Activity that brings on distressing acute fatigue in one person may amount to mild, even pleasant, exertion or another. The difference in fatigue level is due essentially to physical fitness - training of the individual for particular activities under consideration. Thus, a good walker or dancer may soon become fatigued when running or swimming hard. The key, then, to controlling acute fatigue is sufficient training in the activities to be engaged in other to prevent premature and undue fatigue. Knowing one's limits at any given time is also important as a guide to avoiding excessively fatiguing exertion and to determining what preparatory training is necessary.

Chronic fatigue refers to fatigue that lasts over extended periods, which is in contrast to acute fatigue, which tends to be followed by a recovery phase and restoration to "normal" within a more or less brief period of time. Chronic fatigue may be due to any and a variety of medical conditions, ranging from disease to malnutrition (such conditions are the concern of the physician who, incidentally, should evaluate all cases of chronic fatigue to assure that a disease condition is not responsible). It may also be due to psychological factors such as extreme boredom and/or worry over an extended period about having to do what one does not wish to do.

Rest and sleep are essential to a good life, for they afford the body the chance to regain its vitality and efficiency in a positive way. Learning to utilize opportunities for rest and sleep may add years to our lives and zest to our years.

Rest

In general, most people think of rest as just "taking it easy." A chief purpose of rest is to reduce tension so that the body may be better able to recover from fatigue. There is no overt activity involved, but neither is there loss of consciousness as in sleep. Because the need for rest is usually in direct proportion to the type of activity in which we engage, it follows naturally that the more strenuous the activity, the more frequent the rest periods should be. A busy day on the job or an outing may not be as noticeably active as a game of tennis, but it is the wise person who will let the body dictate when a rest period is required. Five or ten minutes of sitting in a chair with eyes closed may make the difference in the course of an active day. For older people a half hour after meals and at other intervals during the day may be needed. The real effectiveness of rest periods depends largely on the individual and her ability to let down and rest.

Sleep

Sleep is a phenomenon that has never been clearly defined or understood but an old Welsh proverb states that "disease and sleep are far apart." It is no wonder that authorities on the subject agree that sleep is essential to the vital functioning of the body and that natural sleep is the most satisfying form of recuperation from fatigue. It is during the hours of sleep that the body is given the opportunity to revitalize itself. All vital functions are slowed so that the building of new cells, and the repair of tissues can take place without undue interruption. This does not mean that the body builds and regenerates tissue only during sleep, but it does mean that it is the time that nature has set aside to accomplish the task more easily.

The body's metabolic rate is lowered, some waste products are eliminated, and energy is restored.

Despite the acknowledged need for sleep, a question of paramount importance concerns the amount of sleep necessary for the body to accomplish its recuperative task. There is no clear-cut answer to this query. Sleep is an individual matter, and the usual recommendation for adults is eight hours of sleep out of every 24, but the basis for this could well be one of fallacy rather than fact. There are persons who can function effectively on less sleep, while others require more. No matter how many hours of sleep you get during the course of a 24-hour period, the best test of adequacy will depend largely on how you feel. If you are normally alert, feel healthy, and are in good humor, you are probably getting a sufficient amount of sleep. The rest that sleep normally brings to the body depends to a large extent upon a person's freedom from excessive emotional tension, and ability to relax. Unrelaxed sleep has little restorative value, but learning to relax is a skill that is not acquired in one night. (It is interesting to note that a report[4] in February 2002 proclaimed that contrary to popular belief, people who sleep six to seven hours a night live longer, and those who sleep eight hours or more die younger. This work quickly provoked a great deal of caution and criticism among experts on sleep, mainly because sleeplessness produces health consequences that this study failed to measure.)

Is loss of sleep dangerous? This is a question that is pondered quite frequently. Again, the answer is not simple. To the normally healthy person with normal sleep habits, an occasional missing of the accustomed hours of sleep is not serious. On the other hand, repeated loss of sleep night after night, rather than at one time, apparently does the damage and results in the condition previously described as chronic fatigue. The general effects of loss of sleep are likely to result in poor general health, nervousness, irritability, inability to concentrate, lowered perseverance of effort, and serious fatigue. Studies have shown that a person can go for much longer periods of time without food than without sleep. In some instances successive loss of sleep for long periods have proven to be fatal. Under normal conditions, however, a night of lost sleep followed by a period of prolonged sleep will restore the individual to her normal self.

Theories of Sleep

Throughout the ages many theories about sleep have been advanced. The ancient Greeks believed that sleep was the result of the blood supply to the brain being reduced. A later idea about sleep was based on the research of the Russian scientist Ivan Pavlov. That is, that sleep was an aspect of the *conditioned reflex.* According to this theory the brain is "conditioned" to respond to any stimulus to become more active. And, the brain can develop the habit of reacting to certain stimuli with the slowing down of the activity. This means that when one is in an environment associated with sleep (bedroom) the brain gets a signal to start to slow down and finally one goes to sleep.

This theory was followed by one that suggested that chemical wastes accumulating in the body during waking hours tend to drug the higher centers of the brain, ultimately causing the slowing down of the brain and therefore sleep.

In more modern times scientists are of the opinion that sleep occurs in cycles and in each of these cycles, which are one and one-half to two hours in length, a sleeper uses about three-fourths of this time in what is called S sleep. This is concerned with what are referred to as Delta brain waves in which one is in deep sleep. The second state is known as D sleep. At this time one may be in deep sleep but at the same time some parts of the nervous system are active and there is *rapid eye movements* (REM). The theory is that *S* sleep restores the body physically and D sleep restores it psychically. As we get older, there is an increase in the amount of REM and deep sleep decreases.

Memory, Brain Function and Sleep

With regard to memory and brain function, a survey[5] of more than 1,000 adults revealed that few understood the important role that sleep plays in maintaining normal daily brain functions, especially memory. Almost half were under the impression that sleep allows the brain to rest. Actually, some parts of the brain may be more active when one is sleeping. While asleep, the brain classifies and prioritizes all this accumulated information, and files it away so that it can be readily retrieved. This process begins with a retrospective review of the day's events, and traveling back in time, so that by morning, one may be immersed in childhood memories.

In addition to memory, sleep is also critical in maintaining concentration, learning and performance skills. The majority of those surveyed admitted that their mental capabilities suffered when they did not sleep well. In those that said that lack of sleep affected them more mentally than physically, 40 percent cited increased stress as their greatest problem, and this was particularly true for women. Sleep has also been shown to improve the ability to learn repetitive tasks, like typing or riding a bike.

When one does not get enough sleep, the ability to move information from short term memory to long term storage becomes impaired. For example, students who sleep several hours before cramming for an examination, retain much more information than those who do not. If one needs to resolve a problem, or make an important decision, "sleeping on it" is probably a good idea.

Sleep and Stress

As mentioned previously, millions of people suffer from some sort of sleep disorder. Millions also have periodic insomnia and this condition is frequently stress related. Sleep deprivation for many is due to excessively long work hours, rotating shifts, last minute preparation for meetings, and unexpected events such as the loss of a close family member.

Working parents may not get enough sleep because of the stress of hectic schedules, or the need to awaken frequently for child care duties.

Stress is the leading cause of temporary insomnia, and chronic insomnia is common in almost every patient with persistent depression, which is often stress related. Just as stress is a major cause of insomnia, lack of sleep is an important source of stress for many individuals. In addition to irritability and fatigue, chronic sleep deprivation can contribute to many disorders. These in turn generate additional stress that interferes with sleep. Finally, in April 2003 the National Sleep Council reported[6] that 66 percent of the people lose sleep because of stress. This was an increase from 51 percent in the previous report.

Getting a Good Night's Sleep

There are various recommendations that could be made about getting a good night's sleep, and there are many conditions that tend to rob the body of restful slumber. Most certainly, mental anguish and worry play a very large role in holding sleep at bay. Some factors that influence the quality of sleep are hunger, cold, boredom, and excessive fatigue. In many instances these factors can be controlled. We need to think of this in two ways; that is, in terms of things *not* to do as well as things *to* do. Although hunger could be an influence on quality of sleep, at the same time overeating near bedtime can interfere with sleep. Being "too full" can possibly cause digestive problems and keep one awake. On the other hand, a little warm milk can often serve as a suitable tranquilizer.

It is generally recommended that one not have any food containing caffeine several hours before retiring. The same can be said for alcoholic beverages. Although it may make you feel drowsy, at the same time the quality of sleep is likely to be disturbed.

An important factor about getting a good night's repose is the sleep environment. This means that conditions should be comfortable for satisfying sleep. We often hear about "good sleeping weather," which really means having the room at a suitable temperature. A general recommendation is that the room temperature be between 65 and 68 degrees Fahrenheit. However, this is an individual matter and one can adjust to the temperature found to be the most suitable.

It has been found that a more or less specific routine should be practiced. For one thing, it is a good idea that the process be the same each night, and should begin at the same hour, leading to repose at about the same time. If your bedtime is normally 10 o'clock, your preparation should perhaps begin as early as 9:30 and possibly by 9 o'clock. You might wish to break off what you are doing at least one-half hour before the fixed time to retire.

The importance of sleep as a goldmine of research is evidenced by the fact that there is an organization called the Association of Professional Sleep Societies, and there are some 150 accredited sleep centers throughout the country.

Understanding the complex nature of sleep may be the province of scientists and other qualified experts, but an understanding of the value of sleep is the responsibility of everyone.

Chapter 7

STRESS AMONG WOMEN IN BUSINESS AND INDUSTRY

Innumerable authoritative sources have proclaimed that job stress is one of the nation's leading adult health problems. According to the United States Bureau of Labor Statistics, stress at the worksite is affecting an astonishing number of people. It is estimated that well over one-fourth of the American workforce is afflicted in some way by job stress. Because of this, costs to employers can reach up to hundreds of billions of dollars annually in absenteeism, reduced output, and poor workmanship. Added to this is the fact that job stress can be the cause of a large number of health-related matters.

The problem of job stress is not restricted to the United States; there is no question that it has reached global epidemic proportions. This concern has been demonstrated by the fact that the International Labor Office issued a 275-page publication on the subject. This comprehensive report titled *Preventing Stress at Work* examined the problem of job stress in numerous occupational pursuits throughout the world.

As far as women are concerned, they have always worked – and worked hard – particularly in the home and in the early history of our country, on the farm. In fact, women were sometimes referred to as "the second mule" when plowing needed to be done. Although women have always worked outside the home to some extent, it might have really started in earnest with "Rosy the Riveter" during World War II. Actually, during this time women on the homefront were one of the most important factors in the success of the war effort.

In modern times the status of women in the work place has changed radically. Nonetheless, severe gaps still remain between the sexes in the workplace. For example, for equal work women received about three-fourths of the amount of pay as their male counterparts. A more favorable statistic, reported in late fall 2002, is that women held 15.7 percent of corporate office positions at large United States public companies, up from 8.7 percent in 1995.[1]

AN OVERVIEW OF STRESS IN THE WORKPLACE

There are many stress-related conditions connected with one's job, and it is well known that some kinds of employment are highly stressful, while others are relatively stress free. Various studies comparing groups have indicated that those in highly stressful occupations tend to have a higher incidence of serious diseases, possibly resulting from stressful conditions on the job.

Perhaps the secret for avoiding many serious diseases lies in attempting to obtain a position of employment where one can deal with stress levels required in that position. The late President Harry Truman characterized this situation with his often-quoted statement, "If you can't stand the heat, stay out of the kitchen." In this particular regard, it has been shown that persons with low confidence in their competencies are likely to seek relatively secure and undemanding occupations, while those with high self-confidence are more likely to seek more demanding occupations.

There seems to be no question that job stress has reached worldwide epidemic proportions, and various surveys bear out the fact that job pressures represent a leading source of stress for adult Americans and that the problem has escalated progressively over the past several years. Similar problems exist all over the world to such an extent that it is now considered to be a worldwide problem. No particular occupation appears exempt. Waitresses in Sweden, teachers in Japan, postal workers in America, bus drivers in Europe, and assembly line workers everywhere are showing increasing signs of job stress.

The nature of job stress varies with different occupations, but affects workers at all levels. Following are some of the major sources.

1. Inadequate time to complete a job to one's satisfaction.
2. Lack of a clear job description or chain of command.
3. Little recognition or reward for good job performance.
4. Lots of responsibility, but little authority.

5. Inability to work with superiors, co-workers, or subordinates because of basic differences in goals and values.
6. Inability or lack of opportunity to voice complaints.
7. Lack of control or pride over the finished product.
8. Insecurity caused by pressures from within or without due to the possibility of takeover or merger.
9. Prejudice because of age, gender, race, or religion.

Management Style and Stress

It should be mentioned that among the sources of job stress listed above, many of them apply to management style. By and large a higher level of job satisfaction is likely to prevail when there is a management style that involves human relations rather than one that is autocratic in nature. This is borne out by a number of studies some of which are reported here.

A Northwestern National Life Insurance study[2] once recommended several suggestions for decreasing employees' stress in order to reduce the incidence of stress-related illness, disability, burnout, or resignation. Companies were advised to facilitate communication among employees and between management and employees; minimize personal conflicts on the job; let employees have adequate control over how they do their work; ensure adequate staffing and expense budgets; support employees' efforts; give employees competitive personal leave and vacation benefits; reduce the amount of red tape that employees must deal with; and recognize and reward employees' contributions.

The effect of participatory action research (PAR) was examined by Catherine Meaney[3] in two plants with divergent management styles, one cooperative and the other using top-down, traditional hierarchical management. (PAR) involved researchers, management, and union representatives in the process of joint problem solving. It was found that PAR involvement improved employee participation in decision making in both contexts, increasing co-worker support and decreasing strain in the traditional plant, and improving employee perceptions of management's openness to suggestions in the cooperative plant.

With regard to women managers, a Gallop telephone poll[4] of 251 women managers and 251 women non-managers found that half of the managers and one-third of the non-managers were frequently bothered by stress. A recent change in working conditions was cited as one of the leading causes of stress among working women. More than 33 percent of the women surveyed identified overwork as a cause of stress. Pay inequity was identified by 27 percent as a major source of stress.

In closing this section of the chapter it seems important to reexamine the traditional concept of the *boss* as conceived by Henry Sims and Charles Manz[5] in their book, *Business without Bosses: How Self-Management Teams are Producing High Performing Companies*. These authors maintain that organizations of the 21st century will rely on self-managing teams and that such teams are coming to the forefront as a critical factor in survival. They assert that a few years ago only 250 manufacturing plants in the United States were using such teams. That number is low in terms of percentages, and more recent estimates would probably indicate the number of companies using teams to be nearing 50 percent.

Although the team approach displaces bosses, it does not eliminate the need for leaders, but these leaders are determined by the teams rather than having a supervisor thrust upon them. It could be that employees do not need bosses continuously staring over their shoulders, telling them what to do, and chewing them out for what they have done wrong. By organizing people into teams and equipping them with what they need in order to do the job themselves, companies can do business without bosses.

In order for self-managing teams to be effective the concept must be embraced by executives who are interested in being competitive. In addition to that, the executives must fine tune the concept to make it work for their organization.

Although one may support the team concept, it should also be recognized that there are challenges in bringing self-management teams into existence. But once in place they seem to be very effective. In fact, it is likely that productivity can be 30 to 50 percent better than in traditional work-groups. Therefore, it seems logical to assume that such an organizational practice could go a long way in reducing stress among corporate employees.

Workers' Compensation Claims Due to Stress

The growing number of job stress problems has resulted in a large increase in workers' compensation awards for such conditions. Rulings vary from state to state on mental-physical, physical-mental claims. All agree that if a physical injury on the job results in an emotional disorder then it is work related. Many states also recognize the opposite possibility, such as a heart attack due to a mental trauma or a stressful relationship with a supervisor.

However, it is the third type of stress case, the mental-mental type that is increasing. In such instances, the worker claims that a mental disorder like depression or anxiety is due to some stressful job problem or even fear of unemployment.

One of the fastest growing segments of workers' compensation claims for job stress is what is known as *repetitive stress injuries*. They are manifested by complaints of soreness and tenderness of the wrists and fingers due to repetitive trauma, especially in computer operators, whose performance may be unknowingly monitored by superiors. One such ailment, *carpal tunnel syndrome*, is characterized by numbness and weakness of the hand due to prolonged pressure on the palm from keeping the wrist in a cocked position from constant typing.

This is not of recent origin because some years ago in studying computer-related stress problems among women, John C. Bruening[6] found that because of the pressure and demands caused by the growth of modern office automation and technology, an increasing number of women in secretarial or clerical positions find themselves in stressful environments. Stress dimensions found in computer mediated work included: (1) job organization factors, (2) physical work station design, (3) environmental and lighting factors, and (4) the interaction of the characteristics of the individual's personality with the characteristics of the job.

Unions are increasingly educating members about their rights to compensation for job stress. In addition, physicians, legislators, attorneys, and judges are becoming more familiar with relationships between stress and illness.

The following list of samples of situations concerned with various aspects of workers' compensation claims that are related to job stress was made available to me by Dr. Paul J. Rosch, President of The American Institute of Stress.

1. In New York City the relationship between job stress and heart attack is so well acknowledged that any police officer who suffers a heart attack on or off the job is assumed to have a work-related disability and is compensated accordingly.

2. Several years ago the Missouri State Division of Employment Security awarded benefits to a former automobile assembly line worker who quit his job simply because of "assembly blues."

3. Courts in at least six states have ruled that emotionally ill employees deserve compensation for "stress accumulated gradually on the job."

4. In Michigan a secretary became hysterical when her boss constantly criticized her for going to the bathroom too often. She received $7,000 and her attorney appealed to get a larger amount.

5. A Maine state trooper, whose duties involved cruising around a quiet rural area, became severely depressed because he was on call 24 hours a day. He claimed that his sex life deteriorated because he never knew when the phone would ring. The case was settled out of court for $5,000.

6. In a Federal Employee Liability Act decision the jury awarded more than $300,000 to an employee who claimed that fear of contracting asbestos-related disease caused him severe stress and anxiety.

7. In California over a 10-year period there was a 700 percent increase in workers' compensation claims for mental stress. Even a judge received an award by claiming that he suffered a stroke from overwork because of an increased caseload of workers' compensation claims.

It is possible that this problem could become so serious that the phenomenal escalation of workers' compensation awards for job stress could possibly threaten to bankrupt the system in some states.

Measuring and Evaluating Job Stress

Increasing concerns about the adverse health effects of job stress have mandated the need to develop scientific methods to measure and evaluate this complex problem. Various questionnaires and rating scales have been developed to study stress in specific occupations, particularly in health care work environments. General measures are often used to rate such things as depression, anxiety, and expression of anger. *The Maslach Burnout Inventory* measures perceptions of professional-client interactions in terms of emotional exhaustion, depersonalization, and personal accomplishments. Attempts to measure job stress and strain in physicians and nurses have resulted in the development of the *Work Related Strain Inventory.* This originally consisted of 45 statements designed to reflect stress-related symptoms reported in health professionals. This was based on a combination of other measures such as the *Physician Stress Inventory, Self-Rating Depression Scale, Social Support Measures,* and *Social Desirability Scale.* It has been refined into an 18-item questionnaire with the assigned items being accorded relative weights of significance, utilizing both reverse or positive scoring. Finally, there is my own *Humphrey Stress Inquiry Form* that can be adapted for use in any specific situation. This instrument which has a reliability coefficient of .90, has been used to collect significant portions of the data reported in this book.

STRESS INDUCING FACTORS FOR WOMEN IN BUSINESS AND INDUSTRY

Stress in business and industry encompasses all manner of individuals from blue collar workers to corporate chief executive officers. None are immune to the potential ravages of stress, with stressors abounding at all levels of the work force.

Over a period of years I have studied stress-inducing factors at all levels for both men and women including blue collar workers, office personnel, managers, and the highest level of corporate executives. I have replicated this work at five-year intervals with the most recent being in 2003.

In the discussions that follow, I will report some of my findings about stress-inducing factors encountered by women on the job in business and industry. These results include a combination of many different populations of workers and included among them are office workers, business executive, various kinds of draftsmen, civil servants, and blue collar workers. I have separated the stressors into four classifications: (1) conditions concerned with facilities, equipment, and supplies, (2) conditions concerned with time factors, (3) conditions concerned with general organizational factors, and (4) conditions concerned with superiors (boss types).

Conditions Concerned with Facilities, Equipment, and Supplies

Slightly more than one-fourth of the women surveyed identified stress-inducing factors in this classification. In the present context, *facilities* are considered to be all of those things that, in one way or another, involve the physical plant and surrounding areas. *Equipment* refers to those kinds of materials that are not as permanent as facilities such as various kinds of machinery. *Supplies* are those materials used almost daily, and are expended over a relatively short period of time. These include an enormously large range of materials such as paper, pencils, and the like.

About 60 percent of the respondents considered deficiencies in equipment as stress inducing. Twenty-five percent identified physical conditions, such as lack of repairs, poor lighting, poor room temperature, and unkempt facilities, as causes of stress. Thirteen percent referred to lack of facilities as a cause of stressful conditions.

Conditions Concerned with Time Factors

About 50 percent of the respondents found that various factors relating to time were a serious cause of stress. Of this number almost three-fourths said they were put under stress because of insufficient time for planning. About half of the workers who identified the time factor as stress inducing simply said there was just not enough time in the day for them to do the kind of job expected of them. Because of this, it became necessary for them to take work home. Interruptions for various reasons were considered by 25 percent to be an unnecessary infringement on their time. Those in this category also complained that it took a great deal of time to get things back on an even keel because of such interruptions. (This area is a much greater concern for women than men because of additional duties in the home.)

Conditions Concerned with General Organizational Factors

Responses of about one-half of those surveyed were directed to stress-inducing factors in this general classification. Forty percent of this total considered *record keeping* practices to be an important cause of stress. Included among record keeping chores were too many forms and too much red tape, unnecessary paper work, and other assorted tasks that could be placed in the general classification of "busy work."

Twenty-five percent felt that *unreasonable deadlines* were a cause of stress, and they felt that they were victims of the "get in yesterday" syndrome. Fifteen percent considered *excess meetings* as stress inducing mainly because such meetings were often poorly organized and rarely served any constructive purpose. The remaining respondents who identified stress-inducing factors in this general classification named as stressful such concerns as being asked to perform duties unrelated to the job. (Secretaries who are required to make and serve coffee.)

Actions of "Boss Types" That Induce Stress

Boss types are considered to be those who are an employee's immediate superior, such as a supervisor, foreman, department head, or administrator. The responses were subclassified into the three broad areas of *administrative practices, administrative incompetence,* and *personality conflicts.*

About forty five percent of the respondents felt that administrative practices were a serious cause of stress. Twenty percent believed that some of the reports they were asked to prepare for their superiors were mostly busy work and did not serve the purpose for which they were allegedly intended. Fifteen percent cited faulty evaluation procedures used by superiors as putting them under undue stress. They identified such practices as being unfair evaluation, lack of recognition of qualified workers, failure on the part of superiors to "weed out" poor workers, and in general, evaluation procedures that were variously lacking in validity. Ten percent considered autocratic tactics of an administrator as stress inducing and generally expressed this in terms of "the boss whose ideas are the only ones." In this particular regard, and as mentioned previously, studies have shown that authoritarian approaches produce more stressful situations for employees than do human-relations strategies for leadership.

For 30 percent of the respondents administrator incompetence was a serious stress-inducing factor. The most noteworthy concerns of employees were expressed in the following ways:

The boss who:
- tries to control rather than help;
- is of little help with most of my problems;
- does not understand the working situation;
- has had no personal experience on the job;
- does not understand the demands of the job.

Almost one-third of the employees considered certain personality conflicts as being stress inducing. Chief among these was inability to communicate with the boss. This was closely followed by complaints such as:

- The boss has a bad feeling toward me;
- There is an incompatible relationship because of petty demands;
- The boss interferes too much;
- The boss is unfair in dealings with employees;
- The boss who is out to get the workers.

(Later in the chapter I will discuss stress-inducing factors for bosses.)

STRESS AMONG BLUE COLLAR WORKERS

It is difficult to determine when the term *blue collar* originated. It might have been at the time when workshirts were supposed to be blue in color and dress shirts white. Most dictionary definitions of the term refer to it as the class of wage earners whose duties call for the wearing of work clothes or protective clothing.

One might think that the so-called blue collar worker does not suffer much stress because she does not have the same degree of responsibility as superiors. However, this is not necessarily the case and a few studies and authoritative pronouncement bear out this contention. Some of this early work is reported here.

One study[7] took into account psychological and physiological stress responses during repetitive work at an assembly line. This concerned the relationship between the perceived stress of workers and their physiological responses to stress in a work situation characterized by repetitive, monotonous, manual work at a Volvo plant in Sweden. Psychological and physiological data were obtained from self-reports assessing variables, such as work demands, time pressure and mood, as well as measurements of catecholamine and cortisol excretion, and of systolic and diastolic blood pressure and heart rate. The findings showed that the workers perceived their work in the assembly line as being monotonous and repetitive, with lack of control and low skill requirements characterizing the work situation. It was also found that workers experienced work demands consistent with the level of physiological arousal induced by the work situation. It was concluded that environmental stress at the assembly line is reflected in health-related physiological responses and that quantitative self-reports of regular workers on perceived stress are closely related to these physiological responses.

Another study[8] examined occupational stress and cardiovascular reactivity in blue collar workers. An analysis was made of the influence of chronic occupational stress on heart rate and blood pressure during a standard mental stress test in a sample of workers from steel and metal-processing plants. Three indicators to measure occupational stress were examined: cumulated workload, worsening of job conditions, and high demand and low job security. The subjects reacted to the mental stress test with reduced cardiovascular responsiveness. These effects persisted after adjustment for relevant factors that could have influenced the results, such as age, smoking, and hypertension. It was concluded that cardiovascular reactivity during experimental tasks should be considered to be not only a possible predictor of future cardiovascular risks but also an outcome of an individual's exposure to chronic stress.

An interesting aspect of blue collar workers is that approximately 20 percent of the work force in the United States is on a *shift* schedule. In this regard one report[9] suggested that shift changes lasting more than a week may result in subtle physiologic problems dealing with readjustment of body temperature and wake-sleep cycles. Almost half of such workers reported disturbances in the amount of sleep they were able to get, as well as the quality of sleep. Other problems were related to changes in eating habits because of altered appetite and digestive complaints. Even more significant were reports of psychological problems dealing with relationships between family and friends, disruption of social activities, and sexual relations. There are a variety of conflicting opinions concerning the influence of frequent shift changes on job accidents. Individuals over the age of 50 seem to be particularly susceptible to work shift related complaints.

My own studies of how female blue collar workers cope with stress are of interest. A relatively small number engaged in organized *physical exercise* to cope with stress. For the most part they felt that they received enough physical activity on the job. However, more than half of them engaged in *recreational activities,* the most popular of which was bowling.

In about 40 percent of the cases they *discussed their problems with others* as a means of coping with stress. Included among those with whom problems were discussed were workmates, boy friends, spouses, and other relatives.

About 15 percent resorted to *drugs and various forms of medication.* They were about equally divided in the use of prescription and nonprescription drugs.

One popular coping technique, particularly among men was the use of alcohol, with about 65 percent engaging in this practice. Many said that "lifting a few" went a long way in helping them relax and thus reduce stress. About 30 percent of women engaged in this practice.

STRESS AMONG "BOSS TYPES"

As mentioned before, boss types are considered to be those individuals who are an employee's immediate superior. This could include all manner of managers up to those who hold high level executive positions.

Although employees identified numerous actions of bosses that induce stress, bosses in turn, named many anxiety-provoking stimuli. One of the greatest stressors for bosses was incompetent workers. Other stress-inducing factors were not too unlike those identified by those they supervised. They felt plagued by a multitude of daily interruptions that deterred completing tasks that had been started. Another stressful condition was one that prevented them from being able to block out time to plan or execute an intended plan because of unexpected circumstances. Many found it stressful when they had to reorganize priorities almost daily. Also inducing stress were too many meetings and too many matters to coordinate. Some women bosses found it stressful when overseeing the work of men.

In closing this chapter, it should be noted that the discussion has been confined pretty much to the private sector. Although there is some overlapping of stressors, there is no question that those in public service can also become seriously stress ridden. For example, it is well-known that many policewomen and female firefighters place their lives on the line daily.

Chapter 8

STRESS AMONG WOMEN IN NURSING

When nurses were first labeled "angels of mercy," they were suitably portrayed. In my own personal experience in teaching courses to undergraduate, graduate, and nurses in service at the University of Maryland School of Nursing and Walter Reed Hospital, I found that the one characteristic that most of them had in common was that of *dedication and caring.* This despite the fact that, for the most part, they are overworked, underpaid, and in too many instances downright "put upon" in one way or another.

At the present time there is a phenomenal shortage of nurses and this is due largely to the two factors of low salary and stress on the job. One report[1] has indicated that by the year 2020 the number of hospital vacancies for nurses will rise to more than 400,000. Moreover, according to my studies about 20 percent of the nurses who drop out of the profession do so because of stress.

A good portion of the content for this chapter was derived from my extensive survey of nurses. The responses were anonymous and of a self-reporting nature. Interest in the study was demonstrated by the high rate of return of 73 percent.

The range of ages of the nurses in the survey was 20 to 67 years with the average being 39 years. Years of experience ranged from one year to 46 years with an average of 14 years. The wide range of nursing specialties is reflected in the following partial list. (There may be some duplication because of different uses in terminology.)

1. Ambulatory Care
2. Bed Control
3. Chemical Dependency

4. Clinical
5. College Health
6. Community Health
7. Critical Care
8. Dialysis
9. Geriatrics
10. Inservice Education
11. Intensive Care
12. Labor and Delivery Room
13. Medical/Surgical
14. Nursing Administration
15. Obstetrics/Gynecology
16. Office Nursing
17. Operating Room
18. Progressive Care
19. Psychiatric
20. Recovery Room
21. Rehabilitation Nursing
22. School Health
23. Staff Nurse
24. Urgent Care
25. Women's Health

Although various estimates place the number of male nurses as high as two percent, none turned up in my sample.

In addition to answering items on the inquiry form, many of the nurse respondents made various interesting comments. Some representative examples of these are as follows:

> I wish you success in your study! If someone could show me how to at least decrease the stress in hospital nursing, I'd go back in a heartbeat and I think a lot of nurses feel that way – it sure would help the shortage. But it seems today everyone is angry – hospital administrators, physicians, patients, their families – and the nursing staff always takes the blame and abuse. No one can work with all that anger!

> My nursing profession is a means to an end. It provides me the financial support for my continuing education and that of my children. My satisfaction is achieved apart from my career, primarily through my family and educational achievements.

The bottom line is not enough nurses due to burnout, demands from families making the hours unrealistic, realistic, working weekends, etc. Other jobs with higher pay and less stress seem more appealing. The higher pay available in some cases for nurses now is not as attractive due to the unrealistic work assignments which are physically and emotionally exhausting and unsafe for patients.

And finally on the need for the study:

I read a lot of articles on "How to Relieve Stress" but not many pertain to nursing specifically.

HOW STRESS IS PERCEIVED BY NURSES

Since the term stress appears to mean so many different things to different people, I considered it appropriate to try to get some idea of nurses' concepts of it. This was accomplished by having my nurse respondents complete   the   following   sentence: Stress   is
_____.

My consideration of how nurses perceived stress focused on the number of times *key* words emerged in the responses. By identifying such key words it was felt that a more or less valid assessment of how nurses conceived of what stress means to them could be identified. The following list shows the percent of time that certain key words occurred. (In all instances where respondents could make more than one choice, the total percentages could go over 100 percent. This applies to other items in the inquiry form as well.)

Anxiety	32%
Emotion	19%
Tension	17%
Pressure	16%
Strain	12%
Frustration	10%
No Key Words	8%

Anxiety

As noted, anxiety was by far the most popular key word used by nurses to define their concept of stress. The following are some representative examples of how nurses used the word anxiety in the concept of stress.

Stress is:
- the result of anxiety;
- anxiety caused by worry;
- those factors which create for the individual or that the individual creates which provide internal anxiety;
- the feeling of anxiety I have over what events may happen to me in the future;
- A state of anxiety created by having to cope with situations beyond my immediate control;
- anxiety produced by lack of skill, energy or time to do a job rewarding and beneficial to my patients;
- those occurrences and situations that cause me anxiety and a feeling of loss of control to some degree;
- the feeling of anxiety due to increased responsibility;
- anxiety caused by racing thoughts of all that needs to be accomplished in too little time;
- any good or bad occurrence that increases anxiety;
- anxiety and responsibility you feel at work that affects you physically;
- anxiety with a feeling of loss of control;
- mental and physical anxiety;
- A cause of anxiety;
- anxiety which can cause a nurse to be successful.

Emotion

The key word appearing second most frequently at 19 percent of the time was emotion. In regard to their stress concept some nurses used the term emotion as follows:

Stress is:
- a bad emotional experience, concerned with emotional upset;
- a situation which causes emotional outburst;

- emotion that influences one negatively;
- an emotional reaction to negative influences in my environment;
- a physical and emotional reaction to a real or anticipated occurrence;
- a condition produced by lack of skill, energy, or time to do a job both rewarding and emotionally and beneficial to my patients;
- the way one reacts physically and emotionally to change;
- emotion induced by life experience;
- emotional response to danger;
- a situation that influences you emotionally;
- an uncomfortable level of demand on either my emotions, my mental abilities, my physical or social self;
- events that subject a person to an altered emotional state.

Tension

The key word appearing third most frequently at 17 percent of the time was tension. Most often those nurses who used the word tension in expressing their concept of stress did so in the following manner:

Stress is:
- tension that is sometimes useful and sometimes detrimental to the individual;
- tension from overwork;
- those conditions which create for one a feeling of tension;
- tension caused by a situation over which I have little or no control;
- mental or physical tension;
- the feeling of increased tension due to demands;
- tension induced by work;
- when I am overcome by tension;
- a lot of tension at one time;
- a combination of several unfavorable conditions that cause tension;
- tension that can cause stomach upset.

Pressure

Closely following tension was the word pressure at 16 percent of the time. Some representative examples of how nurses used the word pressure in describing their concept of stress follow:

Stress is:
—   the result of pressure;
—   pressure from job put on us by management, patients, visitors, and staff;
—   feeling of being overwhelmed, pressured and burned out, and a feeling that control over one's environment is being lost;
—   pressure controlling the physical body and mental attitude;
—   pressure to keep up physically during patient overload;
—   pressure and responsibility felt at work;
—   feeling overwhelmed and pressured with confused thinking;
—   concerned with relieving the pressure you feel;
—   constant pressure on mind and body;
—   the pressure of daily problems;
—   pressure that is harmful to you.

Strain

This key word appeared 12 percent of the time. Examples of how nurses used the word strain in describing stress are listed below.

Stress is:
—   mental or physical strain;
—   a mental or physical strain on a person's coping mechanisms, on the body's ability to adapt to change;
—   the strain resulting from situations encountered in everyday living;
—   a strain on your health;
—   strain brought about because of worry;
—   strain from overwork;
—   strain caused by unknown sources.

Frustration

This key word appeared ten percent of the time when nurses indicated their concept of stress. Some examples of how they used the term frustration are as follows:

Stress is:
- a feeling of frustration caused by having too much to do in too short a time;
- that feeling of increased frustration due to increased responsibility;
- frustration because of not being able to be of more help to patients;
- feeling of frustration if you do a poor job;
- the feeling of frustration you get when things are not going well;
- frustration caused by a mental state;
- frustration that uses up your energy.

In eight percent of the cases none of the above key words were used by nurses in describing stress. Some of these statements follow:

Stress is:
- an internal force created by real, or imagined unmet needs;
- being stretched like a rubber band;
- the feeling of impending danger to complete life threatening demands;
- a feeling of being out of control with no positive;
- direction to turn to;
- a heavy caseload of patients who are very sick, very demanding and who require you to work with little resources and time;
- when you have reached your maximum stimulation threshold;
- where level of coverage and competence is overtaxed to becoming dangerous for patient and nurse;
- being overworked, underpaid and not respected for your abilities.

CLASSIFICATION OF STRESS INDUCING FACTORS

As mentioned previously I was able to obtain firsthand from nurses those factors which induced the most stress. This was accomplished by simply requesting that they identify those factors connected with their job that were most stressful for them. Obviously, this resulted in a huge amount of data. It seemed appropriate to sort out the stressor and place them in what appeared to be the most satisfactory classifications.

The difficulty encountered in attempting to devise a foolproof system for the classification of nurses' stressors should be obvious. The reason for this, of course, lies in the fact that it is practically impossible to fit a given stressor into one exclusive classification because of the possibilities of overlapping. However, an attempt was made to do so, and it should be made clear that the classification on my part was purely arbitrary. With this idea in mind, the following classifications were finally decided upon:

1. Patients.
2. Understaffing.
3. Administration.
4. Coworkers.
5. Time.
6. Physicians.
7. Compensation.
8. Supplies and Equipment.

Patients

It is not surprising that patients are a source of stress for nurses (64 percent). The following wide range of comments made by nurses about patients give some indication of stress that nurses are under when dealing with patients:

- Super-demanding patients.
- When a patient is going from bad to worse.
- Unstable patients not responding to treatment.
- Attempting to help patients when they have no desire to regain health.
- Lack of recognition from patients.
- Mental stress of dealing with geriatric patients and families.
- Lack of respect and compassion from patients.
- Concern about unstable patients.
- High demands placed on me by patients.
- Emotional "neediness" of patients and families.

- Too many patients to care for.
- Dealing with dying patients.
- Dealing with irate family members of patients.
- Terminal patient caseload.
- Inability to cope with patient demands and their families
- Interference with patient care by doctors and the nursing office.
- No one available to help me with patients.
- Number of patients requiring total care.
- Number of times being interrupted when trying to care for patients.
- Being part of the needless suffering of patients as a result of inappropriate use of invasive medical technology.
- Severely ill patients requiring a lot of time.
- High-risk patients.
- No time to communicate with patients.
- Very sick patients all the time.
- Dealing with critical patients in the Intensive Care Unit.
- Too many patients leaving no time for meal break and proper patient care.
- Trauma patients in OR.
- Making important decisions with complex difficult patients.

Understaffing

I have arbitrarily used the term under-staffing to identify this classification of nursing stressors. It has also been described as: work pressure, time pressure, work overload, and inadequate staffing. This classification is a significant source of stress for nurses and about one-half of the nurses in my survey identified it as such. Some of the stressors cited in this classification are as follows:

- Shorthanded and always need more help.
- Too large a patient-nurse ratio in the hospital.
- People lined up at the door with multiple problems (nurse administrator).
- Unstable work environment due to constant changes in staff.
- Concern of losing staff members due to rapid changes taking place in nursing.
- Staff shortage from burnout and hospital economics.

- Poor staffing and shift schedules.
- Making sure all units are adequately staffed (nurse administrator).
- Completion of impossible assignments.
- Inefficient staff organization.
- Too few nurses for the number of patients.
- Too much work to handle.
- Lack of coverage overtaxed to point of becoming dangerous for patients and nurses.
- Unqualified help.
- Lack of coverage due to nursing shortage.
- Untrained help.
- Too many tasks to perform.
- Inadequate staffing is the number one stress factor!!!
- Being overworked.

Administration

Forty-four percent of my nurse correspondents identified certain aspects of administration as stressful. Some of the typical administration-induced stressors included the following:

- Displaced attitudes; that is, paper work over patient care.
- Too little support from hospital administration.
- Administration attitude toward nursing department.
- Having little power in terms of administration.
- Mismanagement.
- Inadequate supervisors.
- Added menial tasks not related to skilled care.
- Lack of control over working environment.
- Paper work when patient's need is great.
- Disciplining difficult staff members (nurse administrator).
- Supervisors lack of knowledge of day-to-day workload.
- Supervisors who do not know how to manage.
- Constant turnover in management.
- Most nursing administrators I've encountered are pleasant and average but not the type of bright person I'd like to see influencing the direction of my profession.
- Administration expecting too much.

- We have a right to expect more loyalty from administrators than they give.
- Not being respected by administrators for your ability.
- Lack of recognition from administration.

Coworkers

Thirty percent of the nurses indicated that they were stressed in some way by their colleagues and coworkers. Following are some examples of how nurses were stressed by coworkers:

- Uncooperative colleagues – late, and not assuming responsibilities.
- Ancillary help inconsistent and not dependable.
- Incompetence of peers and other employees.
- Coworkers who talk nonstop and don't do work.
- Personal conflicts with coworkers.
- Lazy coworkers.
- High demands placed on me by coworkers.
- Unqualified or unmotivated assistants.
- Lack of motivation of other staff members.
- Unprofessional nurses.
- Hostile staff.
- Coworkers who are not flexible.
- When others don't help each other.
- Incompetent uncaring coworkers.

Time

In most studies on occupational stress well over one-fourth of the respondents cite various factors related to time as serious causes of stress. My study of nurses was no exception with 30 percent citing stressors in this classification. Some responses follow:

- Pressure to deliver more than I am able.
- Two or three things that need to be done at once.
- Getting behind in nursing care.
- Long hours.

- Being rushed – too many things to do in a certain time period.
- Having to work all shifts and mandatory overtime.
- Shift rotation.
- Lack of time to do tasks as well as I would like.
- Too much to do in too little time.
- Not enough time to give safe nursing care.
- Irregular hours as compared to the rest of society.

Physicians

Almost one-fourth of the nurses indicated that physicians were a cause of stress. Following are some comments that were made in this regard:

- The doctor's anxiety level.
- Chauvinistic doctors who think they are God.
- Fear of permitting the physician to make a poor choice in patient care.
- Lack of recognition from physicians.
- Irrational and unreasonable MDs.
- Doctors' attitudes.
- Dealing with old time doctors who are very condescending of my knowledge.
- Doctor endangering my self-respect.
- When there is a need to call a physician at night when there is a condition change in a patient.
- Doctors misunderstanding nurse's job.
- Demanding attitudes of doctors.
- Doctors lack of concern for nurses.
- Doctors expecting to have nurses wait on them like maids.
- My frustration is compounded by the fact that unnecessary medical technology is often initiated by a physician to avoid lawsuits down the road.
- Dealing with doctors.

Compensation

Although low salary is a chief cause of nurses leaving the profession, only 12 percent of my respondents found it to be stressful. Most of these were younger nurses who were in the profession for a relatively short period of time.

Supplies and Equipment

Ten percent of the nurses were stressed because of the problem of supplies and equipment. Some of them commented as follows:

- Getting proper supplies and equipment.
- Malfunctioning supplies and equipment.
- Fighting with auxiliary departments like dietary and pharmacy for things you need.

SPECIFIC STRESS REDUCING TECHNIQUES

Nurses were asked to identify those procedures that they found most helpful in relieving them from stress. Some of these techniques were performed as a designated means of reducing stress. Others were engaged in for sheer enjoyment derived from them; nonetheless, the latter type of activities relieved stress as well. For example, six percent of the nurses reported that *having sex* was found to be most helpful in relieving them of stress. Since this is an activity engaged in by practically all of the adult population, this should not be interpreted to mean that it was used only as a stress reduction technique.

A high percentage (69) *engaged in passive recreational activities.* Such activities included reading, listening to music, gardening, and needlework. Sixty-seven percent took part in some form of *physical exercise,* including swimming, jogging, walking, tennis, and other net games. It should be mentioned that physical exercise was engaged in on a more or less sporadic and spasmodic basis.

Two-fifths of the nurses reduced stress by *inducing the relaxation response* through progressive relaxation, biofeedback and meditation. These techniques will be discussed in Chapter 10.

Twenty-four percent resorted to *divine guidance* to reduce stress. Some typical comments in this regard were as follows:

- I trust in my Lord Jesus Christ.
- God and my family.
- Prayer helps to control stress.
- I find relief from stress when I read the Bible.

Another 24 percent used *alcoholic beverages* and this was done moderately, usually with the traditional cocktail before dinner.

Deep breathing was popular with 11 percent and some nurses commented on this in the following manner.

- I pause and take a deep breath at work, forget about it, and slow down before going home.
- I take a deep breath and keep going.
- Although only five percent engaged in *systematic desensitization* as a method of reducing stress, they all found it to be most useful and would recommend it highly to others. This technique is dealt with in detail in Chapter 11 as a form of behavior modification.

Chapter 9

STRESS AMONG WOMEN IN TEACHING

Like nursing, the teaching profession is dominated by women. However the higher the grade level, the more likely men teachers are to be found. Also, in educational administration, men prevail in large numbers. About 90 percent of school superintendents and more than 70 percent of principals are men. In spite of this, it is expected that more and more women will eventually become educational administrators.

In my studies, teachers themselves report that stress is their greatest health problem. Moreover, almost one-fourth of them admit to from poor to fair ability to cope with stress.

UNIQUENESS OF THE PROFESSION

There are numerous factors that make the profession of teaching somewhat unique. And, in years past teachers have been considered a unique breed. In fact, although teachers may be thought of as human beings in modern times, at one time they were considered by some to be somewhat unlike their fellow man (woman) – a "third sex," so to speak. This stereotype has changed appreciably for the better, but nonetheless still persists in certain cases. Although some have designated teaching as the "greatest calling," others subscribe to George Bernard Shaw's "He who can, does, and he who cannot teaches."

Teachers typically make countless decisions every day. They dispense acceptance, rejection, praise, and reproof on a wholesale basis. It is doubtful that many occupations or professions can lay claim to such a "distinction."

It is sobering to think that any one of these many decisions might have either a short or long range positive or negative influence upon a given student.

The average age of teachers is lower than that of most professions. According to my studies, the average is 35 years, and only about 15 percent of teachers have more than 20 years service. About 60 percent of them have said they plan to remain in teaching until retirement. Some reasons given for this are negative student attitude and discipline, incompetent administration, and heavy workload, all of which are stress-provoking conditions.

There are few professions as open to such intense public scrutiny. Perhaps a part of the reason for this is the constant flow of information from students in schools to their parents.

The teaching profession may be one of the highest risk areas as far as violence is concerned. In a year thousands of classroom teachers are physically attacked by students. Moreover, large numbers of teachers will continue to be threatened, harassed and physically assaulted. They will become aware of their personal danger and vulnerability. They will become fearful and develop stress-related symptoms that will affect them psychologically and physically. In fact, the problem of violence has become so pronounced that some teacher education institutions are conducting seminars on the subject of "teacher survival," one purpose of which is to try to provide information on the teacher's role in attempting to cope with violence.

Another more or less unique aspect of the teaching profession is that although a teacher works with a group of students, a high level of sensitivity must be maintained for each individual in the group. The qualified teacher is aware that every student is almost incredibly unique and that he or she approaches all of the learning tasks with his or her own level of motivation, capacity, experience and vitality. The teacher then, by a combination of emotional and logical appeal, attempts to help each student find his or her way through the experience at his or her own rate, and to some extent in his or her own way. All of this, of course, while dealing with a relatively large groups of individuals.

Another factor that tends to set teaching apart from other professions is its criteria for success. In most professions success tends to be measured by the amount of financial remuneration one receives from the job. If this were used as a criterion for success in teaching it is unlikely that many teachers could qualify as being successful.

Over the years there have been numerous attempts to objectively identify those characteristics of successful teachers that set them apart from average or poor teachers. Obviously, it is a difficult matter because of the countless variables involved. It is entirely possible for two teachers to possess the same degree of intelligence, preparation and understanding of the subjects they teach. Yet is it also possible that one of these teachers will consistently achieve good results with students, while the other will not have much success. Perhaps a good part of the reason for this difference in success lies in those individual differences in personality that influence how teachers deal and interact with students. Based upon available research and numerous interviews with both teachers and students, along with my own personal experience, I have found that the following characteristics tend to emerge most often among successful teachers.

1. Successful teachers possess those characteristics that in one way or another have a humanizing effect on students. An important factor that good teachers have that appeals to most students is a sense of humor. One third-grade boy put it this way: "She laughed when we played a joke on her."

2. In practically all cases successful teachers are fair and democratic in their dealings with students and they tend to maintain the same positive feelings toward the so-called "problem" student as they do with other students.

3. A very important characteristic is that successful teachers are able to relate easily to students. They have the ability and sensitivity *to listen through students' ears and see through students' eyes.*

4. Successful teachers are flexible. They know that different approaches need to be used with different groups of students as well as individual students. In addition, good teachers can adjust easily to changing situations.

5. Successful teachers are creative. This is an extremely important factor for teachers at the elementary school level because they deal with a very imaginative segment of the population.

6. Successful teachers have control. Different teachers exercise control in different ways, but good teachers tend to have a minimum of control problems probably because of the learning environment they provide.

It would seem to follow that the more successful a teacher is, the less stress she might encounter. Although this may generally be the case, it is not always necessarily true. For example, successful teachers put themselves under stress by having the courage to think up and work on new ideas rather than maintaining the *status quo*. Successful teachers tend to worry about their students and as a consequence suffer various degrees of undesirable stress because of this. On the other hand, some of this stress may be necessary and desirable, especially when a teacher experiences the exhilaration of knowing that a student has learned thanks to the teacher's willingness to meet a challenging situation.

FACTORS THAT INDUCE STRESS IN TEACHING

My own accumulation of data, alluded to previously, is kept up to date on an ongoing basis. Various aspects of this information will be incorporated into the following discussions. However, it may be appropriate to report on in a general way at this point. The work was extensive in that I surveyed teachers at all levels from the elementary school to university. In addition, most all of the areas of specialization were sampled including teachers of art, music and physical education, as well as teachers of those with learning disabilities. The teachers surveyed included those from the inner-city, suburban, and rural areas.

Inasmuch as this work is essentially concerned with public school teachers below the college level, the greatest emphasis was placed on these. My findings tended to show that, generally speaking, stress-inducing factors did not differ greatly across the combination of areas surveyed. However, certain stress-inducing factors were found to be peculiar to certain segments of the sample. For example, among physical education teachers a unique stress-inducing factor was "complying with Title IX," which deals with integration of the sexes in physical education classes. Unique at the level of college teaching was the stress brought about by what the large majority of college teachers labeled "continuing impingement on academic freedom." Although public school teachers saw administrators and administrative practices as a major stress-inducing factor, this appeared to be much more pronounced among college teachers. Many college teachers felt that they were placed under stress because of what was described generally as a "lack of scholarly achievement among college administrators." The generally prevailing feeling seemed to be that at the college level, administrators were in such positions because of their inability to carry out functions which require scholarly achievement.

General School Working Conditions That Induce Stress

The whole area of general school working conditions that induce stress has been subclassified into conditions concerned with (1) facilities, equipment, and supplies, (2) time factors, and (3) general organization factors.

Facilities, Equipment, and Supplies

Twenty-three percent of the teachers identified stress inducing factors in this classification.

As mentioned previously, *facilities* are considered to be all of those things that in one way or another involve the physical plant and surrounding areas. *Equipment* refers to those kinds of materials that are not as permanent as facilities, such as large pieces of playground apparatus, audio-visual materials, and the like. *Supplies* are those teaching materials that are used almost daily. These include an enormously wide range of materials such as books, workbooks, and all sorts of tools developed by creative teachers. Although teachers did not mention it as being stress inducing, they tend to spend inordinate amounts of their own money for supplies. Some teachers said they did this for the purpose of alleviating stress brought about by insufficient supplies.

Sixty-five percent of the respondents considered deficiencies in school equipment to be stress inducing. Twenty percent identified certain school conditions such as lack of repairs, poor lighting, poor room temperature, and unkempt facilities as a cause of stress. Thirteen percent referred simply to lack of facilities as a cause of stressful conditions.

Time Factors

Twenty-eight percent of the teachers found various factors relating to time to be a serious cause of stress. Of this number, 53 percent said they were put under stress because of insufficient time for planning. As might be expected, this condition was much more prevalent at the elementary school level where in some instances teachers are with students all day long with little or no time at all for any kind of planning. This is, of course, due to the differences in organizational structure of the elementary school as compared to the secondary school.

Twenty-nine percent of the teachers who identified the time factor as stress inducing simply said that there was just not enough time in the school day to do the kind of job expected of them. Class interruptions for various reasons were considered by 18 percent of the respondents to be an unnecessary infringement on the time of teachers. Those in this category also complained that it took a great deal of time to get lessons back on an "even keel" because of such interruptions.

General Organizational Factors

Responses of 49 percent of the teachers were directed to stress inducing factors in this general classification. Forty-four percent of this total considered *record-keeping* practices to be an important cause of stress. Included among record-keeping chores were grading papers, clerical activities, too many forms and too much "red tape," unnecessary paperwork, and other assorted tasks that could be placed in the general classification of "busy work."

Eighteen percent felt that *unreasonable deadlines* were a cause of stress and that they were victims of the "get it in tomorrow" syndrome. Fifteen percent saw abnormal *class size* as being stressful and most of these felt that this involved additional stress concerned with attempting to meet the individual needs of students. Another 15 percent considered excess *meetings* as inducing stress, mainly because such meetings were poorly organized and rarely served any constructive purpose. The remaining eight percent who identified stress-inducing factors in this classification named as stressful such concerns as extracurricular responsibilities, paraprofessional duties and other non-teaching duties, and insufficient in-service training.

Actions of Administrators that Induce Stress

For the most part, stress-inducing factors of administrators were those involving the school principal. This, of course, is to be expected because it is this administrative officer with whom teachers are most likely to come in direct contact. Responses of teachers could be sub-classified into the three broad areas of (1) administrative practices, (2) administrator incompetence, and (3) personality conflicts.

Administrative Practices

About 40 percent of the teachers felt that administrative practices were a cause of serious stress. Eighteen percent believed that preparation of lesson plans for the principal was busy work and did not serve the purpose for which they were allegedly intended. Twelve percent said faculty evaluation procedures used by the principal as evaluation by inspection, unfair evaluation, lack of recognition of good teachers, failure on the part of the principal to "weed out" poor teachers, and evaluation practices in general that were seriously lacking in validity.

The remaining ten percent considered autocratic practices of the principal to be stress inducing and generally expressed this in terms of "the principal whose ideas are the only ones." In this particular regard, there appears to be little solid evidence to support one type of school administrative tactic over another. However, as mentioned in Chapter 7, some studies in industry have shown that authoritarian approaches produced more stressful situations for employees than did human relations strategies of leadership.

Administrator Incompetence

This situation prevailed to a certain extent among teachers in that about 29 percent of them identified stressful conditions in the sub-classification of actions of administrators that induce stress. The most noteworthy concerns of teachers were expressed as follows:

The principal who:
- knows nothing about the reading process;
- controls rather than helps;
- is of little help with the problem children;
- does not understand the classroom situation;
- has not been in the classroom for ten years;
- lacks an understanding of the demands of the job;
- in general is an incompetent, uncooperative, poor administrator;
- avoids major problems so that he can attend to minor ones.

Personality Conflicts

About 31 percent of the teachers considered certain personality conflicts with the administrator to be stress inducing. Chief among these was an inability to communicate with the principal. This was closely followed by such complaints as:

- The principal has a bad attitude toward me.
- There is an incompatible relationship because of petty demands.

- The principal interferes too much.
- The principal is unfair in her dealings with teachers.
- The principal is out to get the teachers.

Actions of Colleagues that Induce Stress

Teachers identified far fewer actions of colleagues that induce stress than they did in other classifications. This is to be expected because at least some degree of *espirit de corps* should prevail among those working toward a common cause. Nonetheless, there were a variety of stress-inducing factors in this classification. Many teachers felt that the teachers' lounge was a place to be avoided because it was used by colleagues to complain about the administration and school conditions in general. Some were stressed by the "freeloader" condition that protected less than dedicated colleagues who were not carrying their share of responsibility. Other factors inducing stress were:

- Lack of responsibility of some teachers for discipline, thus placing this burden on others.
- Weak teachers being assigned few discipline problems so that this responsibility was shifted to more competent teachers.
- Peers being unwilling to work with others.
- Fellow faculty members who are not as impressive as they think they are.
- Indifference of some teachers toward students.
- Odd personalities of some colleagues making so-called "normal" teachers suspect in the eyes of others.

Actions of Parents that Induce Stress

Actions of parents that induce stress in teachers can be classified into three areas: (1) lack of concern of parents for their children, (2) parental interference, and (3) lack of parental support for teachers.

In 45 percent of the cases *lack of parental concern for children* was stressful for teachers. They cited such things as parents not caring when a student did poorly, parents not willing to help their children with school work, a lack of home discipline, and stress placed on teachers by the difficult time they had in getting parents to conferences.

Thirty-two percent of the teachers indicated that *parental interference* is stressful for them. Such interference often was a result of parents having expectations that are too high for their children. This in turn resulted in parental pressure on children, particularly for grades, which may be one of the most serious conditions in our schools today. Incidentally, in this general connection it is interesting to note that attitudes acquired during youth can affect the way an individual reacts to stress as an adult. This may be significant in the case of persons whose families have emphasized performance and achievement to the exclusion of all other characteristics.

The third classification of parental actions causing stress for teachers is that of *lack of parental support,* and 23 percent identified stress-inducing factors in this classification. They were stressed by such factors as not being backed by parents and a poor attitude in general of parents toward teachers.

Student Behaviors that Induce Stress

Of all the stress-inducing factors with which teachers must cope, those that involve student behavior appear to be among the most serious. These behaviors can be classified into the areas of student control and discipline, and students with negative attitudes.

It is no small wonder that 65 percent of the teachers who identified factors in this general area say student control and discipline is a serious stress-inducing factor. This is not surprising because discipline has headed the list of major problems facing our nation's schools in eight of the last nine years of Gallup education polls.

Among the many stress-inducing factors identified by teachers under this classification are the following representative examples:

- Students who argue over test answers.
- Restlessness of students.
- Cheating by students.
- Student insolence.
- Student disobedience.
- Students who reject authority.

It is interesting to make a comparison of teachers' identification of school problems over a 50-year span. During the last several decades teachers have periodically been asked to identify the major problems in our public schools. In the 1940s the following problems were of concern: talking out of turn, chewing gum, making noise, running in the halls, cutting in line, dress code violations, and littering. These problems pale in comparison with the following that were cited half-century later: drug abuse, alcohol abuse, pregnancy, suicide, rape, robbery, and assault.[1]

WHAT TEACHERS ARE DOING TO COPE WITH STRESS

One dimension of my surveys was concerned with what teacher do to cope with stress. It was felt that if such information were available it would provide some guidance for making suggestions and recommendations. These data, derived from teachers at all grade levels and in most of the subject areas, are summarized in the following discussion.

One rather disturbing statistic revealed that 49 percent of the respondents indicated that they were more or less at a loss on how to deal with stress. A common response was to "grin and bear it" and many in this classification felt that this caused more stress. Many others said that they "tried to forget" but this did not help.

In 16 percent of the cases *discussion with others* was a procedure for coping. In the final chapter of the book this practice is stated as a principle of living that teachers might apply in the management of stress. Included among those with whom problems were discussed were peers, spouses, administrators, parents, and psychologists.

Nine percent of the respondents resorted to some sort of *divine guidance* with a majority in this category saying that they prayed and applied the principles that the Bible teaches. It may be of interest to note that a very large number of the responses in this group came from teachers in rural areas.

In seven percent of the cases the important practice of *setting tasks* in the right order of priority was applied by reexamining practices when pressure builds, organizing daily routine, and planning well ahead.

Another seven percent used physical exercise as a method of coping, and this included jogging, biking, and weight training. Most of those in this category were physical education teachers who were perhaps more aware of the value of exercise.

Six percent resorted to drugs and various forms of medication. They were about equally divided in the use of prescription drugs and non-prescription drugs, while a number resorted to the use of alcoholic beverages.

Three percent used recreational activities as a coping measure, and these pursuits included reading at home, leisure work at home, and sports and games. Of the two percent who used *meditation* as a means of coping, all of the respondents reported good success with this technique and recommended it for all teachers. One percent used *progressive relaxation* to cope with stress, although over the years this has been considered to be one of the most important coping procedures.

Chapter 10

INDUCING THE RELAXATION
RESPONSE TO REDUCE STRESS

The term *relaxation response* was introduced by Herbert Benson[1] of Harvard University several years ago and it involves a number of bodily changes that occur in the organism when one experiences deep muscle relaxation. There is a response against "overstress" which brings on these bodily changes and brings the body back into what is a healthier balance. Thus, the purpose of any kind of relaxation should be to induce a relaxation response.

Three ways of inducing the relaxation response are addressed in this chapter. They are: progressive relaxation, meditation, and biofeedback, all of which can be considered as relaxation techniques. It seems important at this point to give attention to the theory underlying these techniques, all of which are concerned with mind-body interactions, and all of which are designed to induce the relaxation response. In progressive relaxation, it is theorized that if the muscles of the body are relaxed, the mind in turn will be quieted. The theory involved in meditation is that if the mind is quieted, then other systems of the body will tend to become more readily stabilized. In the practice of biofeedback, the theoretical basis tends to involve some sort of integration of progressive relaxation and meditation. It is believed that the brain has the potential for voluntary control over all the systems it monitors, and is affected by all of these systems. Thus, it is the intimacy and interaction between mind and body that has provided the mechanism through which one can learn voluntary control over biological activity.

THE MEANING OF RELAXATION
AND RELATED TERMS

In general, there are two types of relaxation – passive relaxation and deep muscle relaxation. Passive relaxation involves such activities as reading and listening to music. In deep muscle relaxation the reality of muscle fibers is that they have a response repertoire of one. All they can do is contract and this is the response they make to the electrochemical stimulation of impulses carried via the motor nerves. Relaxation is the removal of this stimulation.

From the point of view of the physiologist, relaxation is sometimes viewed as being "zero activity," or as nearly zero as one can manage in the neuromuscular system. That is, it is a neuromuscular accomplishment that results in reduction, or possible complete absence of muscle tone in a part of, or in the entire body. A primary value of relaxation lies in the lowering of brain and spinal cord activity, resulting from a reduction of nerve impulses arising in muscle spindles and other sense endings in muscles, tendons, and joint structures.

The meaning of the terms *relaxation, refreshment,* and *recreation* are often confused. Although all of these factors are important to the well-being of the human organism, they should not be used interchangeably to mean the same thing. *Refreshment* is the result of an improved blood supply to the brain for "refreshment" from central fatigue and for disposition of muscles' waste products. This explains in part why mild muscular activity is for overcoming the fatigue of sitting quietly (seventh inning stretch) and for hastening recovery after strenuous exercise (an athlete continuing to run slowly for a short distance after a race).

Recreation may be described as the experience from which a person emerges with the feeling of being "re-created." No single activity is sure to bring this experience to all members of a group, nor is there assurance that an activity will provide recreation again for a given person just because it did so the last time. These are more the marks of a psychological experience. An important essential requirement for a recreational activity is that it completely engross the individual; that is, it must engage her entire undivided attention. It is really an escape from the disintegrating effects of distraction for the healing effect of totally integrated activity. Experiences that produce this effect may range from a hard game of tennis to the reading of a comic strip.

Some individuals consider recreation and relaxation to be one and the same thing, which is not the case. Recreation can be considered a type of mental diversion that can be helpful in relieving tension. Although mental and muscular tensions are interrelated, it is in the muscle that the tension state is manifested.

For many years, various recommendations have been made with regard to procedures individuals might apply in an effort to relax. Examples of some of these procedures are presented in the ensuing discussions. In consideration of any technique designed to accomplish relaxation, one very important factor needs to be taken into account and that is that learning to relax is a skill. It is a skill based on the kinesthetic awareness of feelings of *tonus* (the normal degree of contraction present in most muscles, which keep them always ready to function when needed). Unfortunately, it is a skill that very few of us practice – probably because we have little awareness of how to go about it.

One of the first steps in learning to relax is to experience tension. That is, one should be sensitive to tensions that exist in her body. This can be accomplished by voluntarily contracting a given muscle group, first very strongly and then less and less. Emphasis should be placed on detecting the signal of tension as the first step in "letting go" (relaxing).

You may wish to try the traditional experiment used to demonstrate this phenomenon. Raise one arm so that the palm of the hand is facing outward away from your face. Now, bend the wrist: backward and try to point the fingers back toward your face and down toward the forearm. You should feel some *strain* at the wrist joint. You should also feel something else in the muscle and this is tension, which is due to the muscle contracting the hand backward. Now, flop the hand forward with the fingers pointing downward and you will have accomplished a tension-relaxation cycle.

As in the case of any muscular skill, learning how to relax takes time and one should not expect to achieve complete satisfaction immediately. After one has identified a relaxation technique that she feels comfortable with, increased practice should eventually achieve satisfactory results.

PROGRESSIVE RELAXATION

The technique of progressive relaxation was developed by Edmund Jacobson[2] decades ago. It is still the technique most often referred to in the literature and probably the one that has had the most widespread application. In this technique, the person concentrates on progressively relaxing one muscle group after another. The technique is based on the procedure of comparing differences between tension and relaxation. As previously mentioned, one senses the feeling of tension in order to get the feeling of relaxation.

Learning to relax is a skill that you can develop in applying the principles of progressive relaxation. One of the first steps is to be able to identify the various muscle groups and how to tense them so that tension and relaxation can be experienced. However, before making suggestions on how to tense and relax the various muscle groups there are certain preliminary measures that need to be taken into account.

1. You must understand that this procedure takes time and like anything else, the more you practice the more proficient you should become with the skills.

2. Progressive relaxation is not the kind of thing to be done spontaneously, and you should be prepared to spend from 15 to 20 minutes, or more, at a time in tensing-relaxing activities.

3. The particular time of day is important and this is pretty much an individual matter. Some recommendations suggest that progressive relaxation be practiced daily, sometime during the day and again in the evening before retiring. For many people this would be difficult unless one time period was set aside before going to the job in the morning. This might be a good possibility and might help a person to start the day relaxed.

4. It is important to find a suitable place to practice the tensing-relaxing activities. Again this is an individual matter with some preferring a bed or couch and others a comfortable chair.

5. Consideration should be given to the amount of time a given muscle is tensed. You should be sure that you are able to feel the difference between tension and relaxation. This means that tension should be maintained from about four to not more than eight seconds.

6. Breathing is an important part in tensing and relaxing muscles. To begin with, it is suggested that three or more deep breaths be taken and held for about five seconds. This will tend to make for better rhythm in breathing. Controlled breathing makes it easier to relax and is most effective when it is done deeply and slowly. It is

ordinarily recommended that one should inhale deeply when the muscles are tensed and exhale slowly when "letting go."

How to Tense and Relax Various Muscles

Muscle groups may be identified in different ways. The classification given here consists of four different groups: (1) muscles of the head, face, tongue, and neck, (2) muscles of the trunk, (3) muscles of the upper extremities, and (4) muscles of the lower extremities.

Muscles of the Head, Face, Tongue, and Neck

There are two chief muscles of the head, the one covering the back of the head and the one covering the front of the skull. There are about 30 muscles of the face including muscles of the orbit and eyelids, mastication, lips, tongue, and neck. Incidentally, it has been estimated that it takes 26 facial muscles to frown and a proportionately much smaller number to smile.

Muscles of this group may be tensed and relaxed as follows (relaxation is accomplished by "letting go" after tensing):

1. Raise your eyebrows by opening the eyes as wide as possible. You might wish to look into a mirror to see if you have formed wrinkles on the forehead.
2. Tense the muscles on either side of your nose like you were going to sneeze.
3. Dilate or flare out your nostrils.
4. Force an extended smile from "ear to ear" at the same time clenching your teeth.
5. Pull one corner of your mouth up and then the other up as in a "villainous sneer."
6. Draw your chin up as close to your chest as possible.
7. Do the opposite of the above trying to draw your head back as close to your back as possible.

Muscles of the Trunk

Included in this group are the muscles of the back, chest, abdomen, and pelvis. Here are some ways you can tense some of these muscles.

1. Bring your chest forward and at the same time put your shoulders back with emphasis on bringing your shoulder blades as close together as possible.
2. Try to round your shoulders and bring your shoulder blades apart. This is pretty much the opposite of the above.
3. Give your shoulders a shrug trying to bring them up to your ears at the same time as you try to bring your neck downward.
4. Breathe deeply and hold it momentarily and then blow out the air from your lungs rapidly.
5. Draw in your abdominal muscles so that your chest is out beyond your stomach. Exert your abdominal muscles by forcing them out to make it look like you are fatter than you are.

Muscles of the Upper Extremities

This group includes muscles of the hands, forearms, upper arms, and shoulders. A number of muscles situated in the trunk may be grouped with the muscles of the upper extremities, their function being to attach the upper limbs to the trunk and to move the shoulders and arms. In view of this there is some overlapping in muscle groups *two* and *three.* Following are some ways to tense some of these muscles.

1. Clench the fist and then open the hand, extending the fingers as far as possible.
2. Raise one arm shoulder high and parallel to the floor. Bend at the elbow and bring the hand in toward the shoulder. Try to touch your shoulder while attempting to move the shoulder away from the hand. Flex your opposite biceps in the same manner.
3. Stretch one arm out to the side of the body and try to point the fingers backward toward the body. Do the same with the other arm.
4. Hold the arm out the same way as above but this time have the palm facing up and point the fingers inward toward the body. Do the same with the other arm.
5. Stretch out one arm to the side, clench the fist and roll the wrist around slowly. Do the same with the other arm.

Muscles of the Lower Extremities

This group includes muscles of the hips, thighs, legs, feet, and buttocks. Following are ways to tense some of these muscles.

1. Hold one leg out straight and point your toes as far forward as you can. Do the same with the other leg.
2. Do the same as above but point your toes as far backward as you can.
3. Turn each foot outward as far as you can and release. Do just the opposite by turning the foot inward as far as you can.
4. Try to draw the thigh muscles up so that you can see the form of the muscles.
5. Make your buttocks tense by pushing down if you are sitting in a chair. If you are lying down try to draw the muscles of the buttocks in close by attempting to force the cheeks together.

The above suggestions include several possibilities for tensing various muscles of the body. As you practice some of these, you will also discover other ways to tense and then let go. A word of caution might be that, in the early stages, you should be alert to the possibility of cramping certain muscles. This can happen, particularly with those muscles that are not frequently used. This means that at the beginning you should proceed carefully. It might be a good idea to keep a record or diary of your sessions so that you can refer back to these experiences if it proves necessary. This will also help you get into each new session by reviewing your experiences in previous sessions.

Creative Relaxation

The approach to creative relaxation presented here was developed for the purpose of reducing stress in young children. However, it has gone far beyond this original purpose, since there have been successful applications of it with various adult groups.

The creative relaxation approach suggested here combines a form of imagery and tensing and releasing. One person or a group creates a movement(s) designed to tense and relax individual muscles, muscle groups, or the entire body.

Creative relaxation simply means that there are contrasting creative movements that give the effect of tensing and letting go. An illustration is provided here for a better understanding of the concept.

This example shows the contrast (tensing and letting go) of the muscles of an upper extremity (arm). The leader could start by raising a question such as the following: "What would you say is the main difference between a ball bat and a jump rope?"

This question is then discussed and will no doubt lead to the major difference being that a ball bat is hard and stiff and that a jump rope is soft and limp. The leader might then proceed as follows: "Let's see if we can all make one of our arms be like a ball bat." (This movement is created.) "Now, quickly, can you make your arm like a jump rope?" (The movement is created by releasing the tensed arm.)

The experience can be evaluated by using these questions: "How did your arm feel when you made it like a bat?" "How did your arm feel when you made it like a jump rope?"

Mental Practice and Imagery in Relaxation

Mental practice is a symbolized rehearsal of a physical activity in the absence of any gross muscular movement. This means that a person imagines in her own mind the way to perform a given activity. Imagery is concerned with the development of a mental image that may aid one in the performance of an activity. In mental practice, the person thinks through what she is going to do, and with imagery may suggest, or another may suggest, a condition, and she tries to effect a mental image of the condition.

The use of mental practice in performing motor skills is not new. Research in this general area has been going on for well over half a century. This research has revealed that imagining a movement will likely produce recordable electric action potentials emanating from the muscle groups that could be called up if the movement were to actually be carried out. In addition, most mental activity is accompanied by general rises in muscular tension.

One procedure in the use of mental practice for relaxation is that of making suggestions to one's self. For the most part, in early childhood, we first learn to act on the basis of verbal instructions from others. Later we begin to guide and direct our own behavior on the basis of our own language activities – we literally talk to ourselves, giving ourselves instructions. This point of view has long been supported by research that postulates that speech as a form of communication between children and adults later becomes a means of organizing the child's own behavior. That is, the function that was previously divided between two people – child and adult – becomes an internal function of human behavior. Following is an example of this approach:

I am going to relax completely. First, I will relax my forehead and scalp. I will let all of the muscles of my forehead and scalp relax and become completely at rest. All of the wrinkles will come out of my forehead and that part of my body will relax completely. Now, I will relax the muscles of my face. (continue the procedure from head to toe)

A way imagery can be used to promote a relaxed state is by making *comparative* statements such as "float like a feather," or "melt like ice." Creative persons will be able to think of many such comparative statements to assist "in producing a relaxed'" state.

MEDITATION

The art of meditation dates back more than 2,000 years. Until relatively recent years, this ancient art has been encumbered with religious as well as cultural connotations. In the 1960s, countercultures began using it as a route to a more natural means of living and relaxing. Today, people from all walks of life can be counted among those who practice and realize the positive effects that meditation can have upon the human mind and body.

It is difficult to determine precisely how many people practice meditation. My own studies show that, in most populations, about four or five percent use meditation as a stress-reducing technique. One exception to this is its use among psychiatrists with about 20 percent of them reporting that they engage in meditation to reduce stress. It should not be surprising that physicians who specialize in "disorders of the mind" would themselves practice this technique at a much higher rate than others. As has already been mentioned, the theory of meditation is that if the mind is quieted, other systems of the body will tend to be stabilized more readily.

Although there are many meditation techniques, *concentration* is an important factor contributing to success in most of them. The mind's natural flow from one idea to another is quieted by the individual's concentration. Lowering mental activity may be an easy task, but almost total elimination of scattered thoughts takes a great deal of time and practice on the part of the meditator.

The question that is sometimes raised is: Are sleep and meditation the same thing? Sleep has been likened to meditation, as both are hypometabolic states; that is, restful states where the body experiences decreased metabolism. But meditation is not a form of sleep. Although some similar psychological changes have been found in sleep and meditation, they are not the same and one is not a substitute for the other. In this regard, it is interesting to note that various studies have shown that meditation may restore more energy than sleep.

There have been countless positive pronouncements about meditation from some of the most notable scientists of modern times, who spend a good proportion of their time studying stress. The scientific community has uncovered many of the positive effects that the repeated practice of meditation has upon those who are stress ridden. Various scientific studies have shown that meditation can actually decrease the possibilities of contracting stress-related disorders, and that meditators have a much faster recovery rate when exposed to a stressful situation than non-meditators. Specifically, from a physiological point of view, meditation decreases the body's metabolic rate, with the following decreases in bodily function involved: (1) oxygen consumption, (2) breathing rate, (3) heart rate and blood pressure, (4) sympathetic nervous system activity, and (5) blood lactate (a chemical produced in the body during stressful encounters). Also, meditation tends to increase the psychological ability of those who practice it, as well as reduce anxiety. Research seems to be disclosing that meditation can be a path to better health (later in this chapter some of this scientific inquiry will be examined in more detail).

Types of Meditation

Having made a rather thorough examination of the literature on meditation, I have been able to identify more than 20 meditational systems. Interestingly enough, although there are many meditation techniques, research tends to show that one technique is about as good an another for improving the ways we handle stress.

I have arbitrarily selected four types of meditation for discussion here: (1) Christian meditation, (2) meditative running, (3) strategic meditation, and (4) transcendental meditation.

Christian Meditation

If you ask the average person about meditation the response will ordinarily be that it has something to do with "sitting and thinking," or "engaging in silent prayer." Basically, this is essentially what Christian meditation means. One feels that she is meditating by reflecting upon certain experiences and evaluating certain activities that have taken place in her life.

Meditative Running

Two prominent researchers, Diane and Robert Hales,[3] have reported on a concept that has to do with a combination of meditation and running and what I would describe as meditative running. Although running and meditation seem like completely opposite states – one strenuous and the other serene – both can be considered as paths to altered states of consciousness, and together they can profoundly affect both mind and body. It is interesting that exercisers who meditate as they work out literally change the way their heart and lungs function. They burn less oxygen and use energy more efficiently. It is known that Tibetan monks, using a similar approach and concentrating on a mantra, have run distances of 300 miles over mountain trails in less than 30 hours.

Strategic Meditation

Amarjit S. Sethi,[4] one of my authors in my series on *Stress in Modern Society,* has developed a concept called strategic meditation. He defines it as a process of balancing "calculative thinking" and "non-calculative thinking." In order to give specificity to this concept he has labeled it strategic meditation so that it may be distinguished from other forms of meditation. The meditational process takes place in different contexts, comprising both the facts and the values of a given environment. The study of interactions between facts and values in shaping calculative and non-calculative thinking becomes a process of strategic meditation. It is strategic because meditation examines problems, identifies their nature, and establishes perspective. It is meditational because a person transforms the problem-solving orientation through a focus on both the problem and its solution, and this begins to suggest elements of how an individual processes information in a relatively "problem free context" which has been termed non-calculative. Another term for such a level of consciousness is *playfulness.* The emphasis, in a meditational exercise, shifts from complex calculative and sophisticated decision rules to selective perception, leading to a problem-free context.

In order to practice strategic meditation one needs to develop her own diagnosis of the problem. Problem-solving is utilized as a process of investigating the source of stress, and is integrated as a part of the meditational process. This phase involves perception of the environment, analysis of the problem, and design of alternative solutions. The problem-solving process is integrated with a meditational process.

Transcendental Meditation

Of the various systems of meditation, transcendental meditation (TM) is by far the best known. It was introduced in the United States many years ago by Mararishi Yogi. It is believed that he used the term transcendental (literal meaning of which in "going beyond") to indicate that it projects one beyond the level of a wakeful experience to a state of profound rest along with heightened alertness.[5]

TM involves the repetition of a *mantra* (a word or specific sound) for 15 to 20 minutes daily with the meditator in a relaxed position with eyes closed. Almost without exception those who have practiced TM attest to its positive effects. Although other forms of meditation may have a specific procedure, it is safe to say that most derive in some way from basic TM. The discussion that follows is based on this type of meditation.

A Procedure for Meditating

Presented here is a description of a procedure for meditating that I have personally found to be successful. In addition, many of my students have reported success with its use. However, it should be mentioned that it is pretty much an individual matter, and what may be successful for person many not necessarily be successful for another.

To begin with, there are certain basic considerations that should be taken into account. The following descriptive list of these considerations is general in nature, and the reader can make her specific application as best fits individual needs and interests.

Locate a Quiet Place and Assume a Comfortable Position

The importance of a quiet environment should be obvious since concentration is facilitated in a tranquil surrounding. The question of the position one may assume for meditation is an individual matter. However, when it is suggested that one assume a comfortable position, this might be amended by, "but not too comfortable." The reason for this is that if one is too comfortable there is the possibility of falling asleep, and this of course would defeat the purpose of meditation. This is a reason why one should consider not taking a lying position while meditating.

A position might be taken where there is some latitude for "swaying." This can provide for a comfortable posture and, at the same time, guard against "falling into dreamland." The main consideration is that the person be in a comfortable enough position to remain this way for 15 minutes or so.

One such position would be where you sit on the floor with legs crossed, the back straight and resting on the legs and buttocks. Your head should be erect and the hands resting in the lap. If you prefer to sit in a chair rather than on the floor, select a chair with a straight back. You need to be the judge of comfort and, thus, you should select a position where you feel you are able to concentrate and remain in this position for a period of time.

Focus your Concentration

As mentioned before, concentration is the essential key to successful meditation. If you focus on one specific thing, such as an object or a sound or a personal feeling, it is less likely that your thoughts will be distracted. You might want to consider focusing on such things as a fantasy trip, re-experiencing a trip already taken, a place that has not yet been visited, or a certain sound or chant.

Use a Nonsense Word or Phrase

Some techniques of meditation, such as the popular transcendental meditation, involve the chanting of a particular word (mantra) as one meditates. While the mantra has important meaning for the meditator, I refer to it as a nonsense word because it should be devoid of any connotation that would send one thinking in many directions. This, of course, would hinder concentration, so a nonsense word would be the most effective. Incidentally, I have found in my own personal experience with meditation that the practice of chanting such a word is very effective.

Be Aware of Natural Breathing Rhythm

The importance of natural breathing rhythm should not be underestimated. In fact, some clinical psychologists recommend this as a means of concentrating. One can count the number of time she inhales, and this in itself is a relaxing mental activity.

The Time for Meditation

Since meditation is an activity meant to quiet the mind it is strongly recommended that the practice not be undertaken immediately at the end of the day. At this time, the mind may be in a very active state of reviewing the day's activities. Personal experience of mine suggests a 15 to 20 minute period in the morning and another such period in the evening preferably before dinner, or possibly two hours after dinner.

With the above basic considerations in mind, you should be ready to experiment. To begin with, assume a comfortable position in a quiet place with as passive an attitude as possible. Try to dismiss all wandering thoughts from your mind and concentrate on a relaxed body while keeping the eyes closed. When feeling fairly relaxed, the repetition of the nonsense word or phrase can begin. This can be repeated orally or silently. Personally, I have had good success repeating it silently; that is, through the mind. Repeat your chosen word or phrase in this manner over and over, keeping the mind clear of any passing thoughts. At first, this may be very difficult, but with practice it becomes easier.

After a period of about 15 or 20 minutes have passed, (or less if you wish), discontinue repetition of the word or phrase. Become aware of your relaxed body once again. Give yourself a few moments before moving as your body will need to adjust. For successful prolonged results one might consider continuing the practice two times daily for 15 to 20 minute sessions.

If you have difficulty trying to meditate on your own, it is possible to seek the services of an experienced meditator for assistance and supervision. The recent more widespread popularity of meditation has been accompanied by the establishment of meditation centers for instruction in some communities.

Scientific Evidence Supporting the Benefits of Meditation

Since many people are not aware of the value of meditation and since many others suspect it as being a rather "spooky" procedure, it seems fitting to impress upon the reader that it is a very important area of scientific research.

The phenomenon of meditation is not an easy one to study objectively. One of the primary reasons for this is that it is extremely difficult to control all of the variables inherent in a given situation. For example, the difference in the length of meditation sessions as well as the degree of meditating experience of the subjects sometimes militates against obtaining researchable experimental and control groups. These limitations should be kept in mind when reading the following summary of research findings.

1. Meditation can slow metabolism and thus promote deep rest.
2. In some cases meditation can increase resistance to disease.
3. Meditation has been shown to improve reaction time; thus, it could be speculated that it can help improve coordination of mind and body.

4.   There may be a correlation between meditation and immunity.
5.   In some instances the practice of meditation may improve memory.

Although most studies have shown positive effects of meditation, it is repeated that certain precautions need to be taken into account in interpreting the results, and the reader is reminded again of the limitations that were mentioned at the outset of this discussion.

In closing this section of the chapter, it is reiterated that whether or not one chooses meditation as a technique for stress reduction is an individual matter. At the same time, it might be good to recall that while a relatively small number of those in my surveys used meditation as a means of coping with stress, all such respondents reported great success with the technique and recommended it for others.

BIOFEEDBACK

In the discussion of biofeedback, it should be made clear that we are dealing with a complex and complicated subject. This phenomenon will be discussed in terms of what it is supposed to be and what it is supposed to do. It should be borne in mind that, at least in the early stages of bio-feedback training (BFT), an important factor is that it should take place under qualified supervision. This means that anyone wishing to pursue an interest in, and eventually participate in BFT, should seek the services of an individual who is trained in this area.

The Meaning of Biofeedback

The term *feedback* has been used in various frames of reference. It may have been used originally in engineering in connection with control systems that involve feedback procedures. These feedback control systems make adjustments to environmental changes, such as in the case of a thermostat controlling temperature levels in the home.

Learning theorists use the term feedback interchangeably with the expression *knowledge of results* to describe the process of providing the learner with information as to how accurate her reactions were. Or, in other words, feedback is knowledge of various kinds that the performer received about her performance. With particular reference to motor skill learning, feedback in the form of knowledge of results is the strongest, most important variable controlling performance and learning, and further, studies have repeatedly shown that there is progressive improvement with it, no improvement without it, and deterioration after its withdrawal.

According to Barbara Brown,[6] one of the foremost early authorities on the subject of biofeedback, the terms *feedback* and *control systems* were borrowed by physiologists when they began theorizing about how the functions of the body were performed.

There are numerous ways in which biofeedback can be described. One description could be that it is any information that we receive about the functioning of our internal organs such as the heart, sweat glands, muscles and brain. Another description could indicate that it is a process in which information about our organism's biologic activity is supplied for perception by the same organism. This could be extended by indicating that biofeedback is the monitoring of signals from the body, such as muscle tension and hand warmth, and the feeding of this information back through the use of sophisticated machines to individuals so they can get external information as to exactly what is happening in their bodies.

There are perhaps millions of individual feedback systems in the human body, and information about the external environment is sensed by way of the five senses and relayed to a control center, usually the brain, where it is integrated with other relevant information. When the sensed information is significant enough, the central control generates commands for appropriate body changes.

These senses can also be thought of as the systems of *perception;* that is, how we obtain information from the environment and what we make of it. Learning theorists agree that forms of perception most involved in learning are *auditory* perception, *visual* perception, *kinesthetic* perception, and *tactile* perception. Auditory perception is the mental interpretation of what a person hears. Visual perception is the mental interpretation of what a person sees. Kinesthetic perception is the mental interpretation of the sensation of body movement. Tactile perception is the mental interpretation of what a person experiences through the sense of touch. In this regard, it is common practice among learning theorists to refer to auditory feedback, visual feedback, kinesthetic feedback and tactile feedback.

Biofeedback Instrumentation

We are all aware of the fact that the human body itself is a complicated and complex biofeedback instrument, which alerts us to certain internal activity, as mentioned in the previous discussion. However, on the subject of biofeedback instruments, many students feel that there is still a need for sensitive instruments to monitor physiological and psychological reactivity. Following is a brief discussion of the more widely known biofeedback instruments that are used both for research and therapeutic purposes.

Electromyograph (EMG)

Electromyography is the recording of electric phenomena occurring in muscles during contraction. Needle or skin electrodes are used and connected with an oscilloscope so that action potentials may be viewed and recorded (the oscilloscope is an instrument that visually displays an electrical wave on a fluorescent screen). Before the electromyograph was available, guesswork ordinarily had to be used to try to determine the participation of the muscles in movement. When a muscle is completely relaxed or inactive it has no electric potential. However, when it is engaged in contraction, current appears.

It is believed that EMG training can produce deep muscle relaxation and relieve tension. A person gets the feedback by seeing a dial or hearing a sound from the machine, and she knows immediately the extent to which certain muscles may be relaxed or tensed. A muscle frequently used in EMG training for research and other purposes is the *frontalis* located in the front of the head.

Another important aspect of EMG is that which is concerned with retraining a person following an injury or disease when there is a need to observe small increments of gain in function of a muscle.

Feedback Thermometers

The obvious purpose of feedback thermometers is to record body temperatures. Ordinarily, a thermistor is attached to the hands or fingers. This highly sensitive instrument shows very small increments of degrees of temperature change so that the person receives the information with a visual or auditory signal. This kind of feedback instrumentation has been recommended for such purposes as reduction of stress and anxiety and autonomic nervous system relaxation.

Electroencephalograph (EEG)

The purpose of this instrument is to record amplitude and frequency of brain waves, and it has been used in research for many years. It has also been used with success to diagnose certain clinical diseases. In addition, EEG feedback has found use in psychotherapy, and in reducing stress as well as pain.

An interesting relatively recent horizon for EEG feedback is how it might be involved in creativity and learning. In fact, some individuals involved in creative activity have indicated that they can emerge from the EEG *theta* state with answers to problems that they were previously unable to solve. The theta waves are ordinarily recorded when a person is in a state of drowsiness or actually falling asleep. It is perhaps for this reason that this condition has been referred to by some as "sleep learning." Since it is a state just before sleep, others refer to it as the twilight period or "twilight learning."

Galvanic Skin Response (GSR)

There are several different kinds of GSR instruments used to measure changes in electrical resistance of the skin to detect emotional arousal. This instrument reacts in proportion to the amount of perspiration one emits and the person is informed of the changes in electrical resistance by an auditory or visual signal. One aspect of GSR is concerned with the use of the polygraph or lie detector, which is supposed to record a response that is concerned with lying. GSR feedback is oftentimes recommended for relaxation purposes, reducing tension, improvement of ability to sleep, or for emotional control.

In general, the purpose of biofeedback machinery is to provide accurate and reliable data that will increase one's awareness of how the body is functioning and demonstrate one's influence of her action of the body. Hopefully, this information should be useful in inspiring a person to take an active self-interest in her own well-being. After such information is received, if it has been obtained under the supervision of a qualified person, there may be a given number of sessions arranged for consultation and training. Perhaps the ultimate objective is for the individual to be able to gain control over her own autonomic nervous system.

As popular and well-advertised as biofeedback machinery has become, it is not without its critics who feel that many important purposes can be accomplished without instruments by using the body as its own biofeedback instrument. In general, they identify such factors as: (1) diverse muscle relaxation, (2) change of heart rate and body temperature, (3) change of breathing patterns, (4) decrease of stress and anxiety reactions, (5) mental relaxation, (6) autonomic nervous system relaxation, (7) pain relief for tension headaches, backaches, and other aches and pains, and (8) improved learning ability, including enhancement of concentration and recall.

However, the critics would probably admit that certain biofeedback instruments, particularly EMG, have important application for retraining of patients following disease and injury.

At the present time, it is difficult to unequivocally determine what the future of biofeedback may be. Without question it has influenced our way of thinking with reference to a person being able to possibly control her physiological functions. In view of this, perhaps one of its foremost contributions is that it creates in an individual a feeling of responsibility for her personal well-being.

In conclusion, it is worth repeating that at least in the early stages, the practice of biofeedback training should take place under the supervision of a qualified person. Also, if a disease syndrome is present a physician's referral may be required.

Chapter 11

REDUCING STRESS THROUGH BEHAVIOR MODIFICATION

For purposes of this discussion, *behavior* as it was described in Chapter 2, will be considered as anything that the organism does as a result of some sort of stimulation. The term *modification* means a change in the organism caused by environmental factors. Thus, when the two terms are used together – behavior modification – they are interpreted to mean some sort of change in the way a person has ordinarily reacted to a given stimulus.

It is not uncommon for some individuals to display behavior that directly or indirectly causes stress arousal, either for themselves and/or for the other person(s) toward whom the behavioral action is directed. It is the function of this chapter to provide information that will assist the reader to modify her own behavior for the purpose of correcting or at least improving upon this condition.

In recent years, behavior modification has become so broad in scope that it is used in many frames of reference. It is emphasized at this point that, for purposes here it is not being considered as a variety of psychological and/or psychiatric techniques (therapist-client relations) for altering behavior. On the contrary, the recommendation for use of modification of behavior is confined to its possibilities as a means for individuals to reduce certain stress-connected factors involved in their various environments. This is to say that if a person manifests a behavior that provokes a stressful situation, if she can change that behavior, it could be possible to eliminate, or at least minimize the stressful condition. For example, let us say that if a person constantly uses what others consider to be unwarranted criticism, this can create a problem in social relationships and thus a stressful atmosphere.

In general, the practice of behavior modification involves external assistance as in the case of a teacher or counselor trying to effect a behavior change in a student or a group of students. The major concern here is in the direction of *self* modification with the individual attempting to improve upon her own behavior. Generally speaking, this assumes that a person can develop the ability to increase desirable or appropriate behavior. Of course, this involves self-control, which can be described as manipulation of environmental events that influence one's own behavior for the purpose of changing behavior. Self-control can eventually lead to behavioral self-management, which can be considered as the learning and practice of new habits.

TOWARD AN UNDERSTANDING OF SELF

In order to put an understanding of self in its proper perspective, consideration needs to be given to the basic concept of *self-structure* and *self-concept*. Self-structure is the framework of a particular individual's complex of motives, perceptions, cognitions, feelings, and values – the product of developmental processes. Self-structure is revealed in behavior. One reveals in her behavior the knowledge, skills, and interests acquired, the goals she is seeking, the beliefs, values, and attitudes adopted, the roles learned and the self-concept formed. Thus self-structure is an aspect of behavior.

Among the most relevant and significant perceptions that an individual acquires are those of herself in various life situations; basically, the self-concept is made up of a large number of *percepts,* each of which contains one or more qualities that one ascribes to herself. To be more specific, *self-percept* pertains to sense impressions of a trait one ascribes to herself while *self-concept* consists of the totality of one's self-percepts organized in some sort of order.

PROCESSES OF BEHAVIOR ADJUSTMENT

The term *adjustment* can be described as the process of finding and adopting modes of behavior suitable to the environment or to changes in the environment. Daily living involves a continuous sequence of experiences characterized by the necessity for the human organism to adjust. Consequently, it may be said that "normal" behavior is the result of successful adjustment, and abnormal behavior results from unsuccessful adjustment. The degree of adjustment that one achieves depends upon how adequately she is able to satisfy basic needs and fulfill desires within the framework of the environment and the pattern or ways dictated by society.

As mentioned previously, we tend to think of stress as any factor acting internally or externally that renders adaptation difficult, and induces increased effort on the part of a person to maintain a state of equilibrium within herself and with her external environment. In Chapter 5, the following points were made and are repeated here for purposes of continuity. When stress is induced as a result of the individual's not being able to meet her needs (basic demands) and satisfy desires (wants or wishes), *frustration* or *conflict* results. Frustration occurs when a need is not met; and conflict results when choices must be made between nearly equally attractive alternatives or when basic emotional forces oppose one another. In the emotionally healthy person, the degree of frustration is ordinarily in proportion to the intensity of the need or the desire. That is, she will objectively observe and evaluate the situation to ascertain if a solution is possible, and if so, what solution would best enable her to achieve the fulfillment of needs or desires. However, every person has a "zone of tolerance" or limits for physical, physiological, and psychological stress within which she normally operates. If the stress becomes considerably greater than the tolerance level, or if the individual has not learned to cope with her problems and objectively and intelligently solve them, some degree of maladjustment can possibly result.

SOME GENERAL PROCEDURES FOR SELF MODIFICATION OF BEHAVIOR

Over the past several years a voluminous amount of literature has been published in the general area of behavior modification. Some of this has been directed to school administrators, teachers, counselors, and others for the purpose of utilizing the procedure to produce behavior change in students. As mentioned before, the concern here is with self modification of behavior and literature in this specific area is becoming more abundant.

Although self modification of behavior is considered to be a relatively recent innovation, one report[1] suggests that it was used in the early history of our country by Benjamin Franklin. He is said to have used it to improve upon such virtues as temperance and frugality. He kept a record of the errors he thought he made each day in each of over a dozen virtues. At the end of the day, he would consult the information to get feedback to help him identify those virtues he may have been violating. Of course, in modern times our approach to self modification of behavior is much more sophisticated than that of Franklin, and improvement in procedures is constantly being made.

Whether one is attempting to modify behavior of another (teacher with a student) or trying to modify her own behavior, the general procedures of application are essentially the same. There are certain sequential steps to be taken that involve the following: (1) identification and description of one's behaviors, (2) counting behaviors, (3) attempting to effect a change in behavior, and (4) evaluating the procedures used to change behaviors. The following discussion will take into account some of the important features involved in these various steps.

Identifying Behaviors

The first step in the process is concerned with identification of a behavior that one wishes to modify. This process is also referred to as *pinpointing, targeting,* or *specifying* a behavior. Essentially, this involves trying to define a particular behavior (target) that one wishes to change. This is not always an easy matter because sometimes a person may manifest a behavior that is annoying to others but be completely unaware of it.

When a person is able to identify a behavior and admit that such a behavior may be interfering with social relationships, a strong beginning can be made in the direction of behavioral change. In other words, recognizing that one has a problem is the first prerequisite to solving it.

In many instances, the identification of a behavior emerges when one is dissatisfied with what she is doing. For example, a person may find that she may be performing a behavior she does not want to perform, or that she may not be performing a behavior she wants to perform.

In the discussion that follows, a hypothetical model of self modification of behavior depicts Janet Smith, who is returning to college to take courses for a teaching certificate. She is in the process of student teaching and is currently taking a required course in "The Psychology of Teaching." The reader is asked to think of a personal situation in which she might utilize the procedure shown in the model.

Ms. Smith has been assigned as a sixth grade student teacher. She is also enrolled in the evening required course "The Psychology of Teaching." In one class session on the general topic of "student attention," the discussion focused upon inappropriate teacher response to student behavior. It was brought out that one form of inappropriate behavior is the command given contingent upon the occurrence of a particular student behavior. That is, when there is a noise the teacher commands, "Be quiet!" Or, when students are out of their seats, the teacher commands, "Sit down!" It was also revealed that contingent "sit down" commands actually increase the frequency of standing behavior among students.

Ms. Smith not only recognized that she had been performing this behavior in her student teaching, but that also on occasion it had degenerated into a "shouting match" with students, creating a stressful situation. Inwardly she had been dissatisfied with herself for performing this behavior, but had neglected to do anything about it. Upon learning that this form of behavior could make a bad situation worse, she felt a desperate in need to try to correct it. She had identified an inappropriate behavior and thus, theoretically, was ready for the next step in self-modification of behavior - *counting* behaviors.

Counting Behaviors

The second step is concerned with actually counting how often a target behavior occurs. This means that one obtains a frequency count of the behavior to be improved. If this step is not taken, it is difficult to learn the extent to which the behavior is being performed. Sometimes simply counting a behavior will tend to improve it because the person is becoming more self-aware of the behavior. This is to say that counting a behavior calls one's attention to it and how often it is occurring.

In addition to determining the frequency of a behavior, another aspect of this step is what is sometimes called the *ABC Factor* in the behavior modification approach. That is, *A*ntecedent of the behavior, the *B*ehavior itself, and the *C*onsequence of the behavior. *Antecedent* is concerned with any event that preceded the behavior and *consequence* is what happens as a result of the behavior. Following are some examples of "ABCs of behaviors" that occurred in Ms. Smith's student teaching experience.

Obviously it is most important that a person develop an awareness of antecedents and consequences of behaviors. The main reason for this is that an antecedent gets a behavior started and a given behavior can result in an unsatisfactory consequence, as in the above illustration.

Antecedent	Ms. Smith's behavior	Consequence
Item 1. Student gets out of seat.	Ms. Smith shouts at student to "Sit Down!"	Class laughs at Ms. Smith.
Item 2. Student talks out to another student.	Ms. Smith shouts at student to "Be quiet!"	Student gives Ms. Smith a bored look.
Item 3. Student falls asleep.	Ms. Smith claps hands close to student's ears and awakens him.	Disruption of class by guffaws of other students.

Attempting to analyze an antecedent becomes important in terms of a manifested behavior. That is, why did the antecedent occur in the first place? In the case of the above example, questions such as the following might be raised.

Item 1. Why did the student leave his seat? Was he justified in doing so? Did Ms. Smith react too quickly?

Item 2. Why did a student talk out to another student? Was this a persistent behavior of this particular student?

Item 3. Why did the student fall asleep? Was he ill? Has he been doing this before, or was it the first time?

The information derived from the second step is usually designated as *baseline data*. If the information is valid and the behavior frequency is accurate, the person has a base from which to operate. This means that one should be in a position to see if attempts at improving a given behavior – step three, *changing behavior* – are meeting with satisfactory results.

Changing Behaviors

Any effort to change a behavior that has been identified, described, counted, and recorded is referred to as a *plan of intervention*. The person intervenes with one or more procedures designed to modify the inappropriate behavior. Any plan to replace an inappropriate behavior with an appropriate one involves some sort of reinforcement procedure. Generally speaking, self-reinforcement is concerned with changing behavior through *self-produced* consequences, and these consequences may be overt or covert. Examples are statements to oneself or the acquisition of an item as a reward for one's efforts.

To help in the clarification of step three, let us return to the case of Ms. Smith. It will be recalled that she was dissatisfied with her constant shouting and criticism of some of her sixth graders. She had gone through steps one and two by identifying a target behavior and gathering information in the way of frequency of occurrence, along with an analysis of antecedents and consequences.

In her course in "The Psychology of Teaching" one of the topics for discussion was "teacher praise versus teacher criticism" in dealing with students. Recognizing that her behavior with her sixth grade class was predominantly characterized by criticism, she took as her term project a study of these two factors – teacher praise and teacher criticism. Her investigation into the literature on the subject revealed the following information.

1. Teacher behavior in such forms as smiles, praise and words of encouragement, if made contingent upon an appropriate student behavior tend to increase the frequency of that behavior; therefore, these forms of teacher behavior operate as reinforcers for many student behaviors (this suggested to Ms. Smith that she might consider minimizing criticism of inappropriate student behavior and maximizing praise for appropriate behavior).

2. Teacher behavior that ignores inappropriate student behavior can be effective in diminishing that behavior. This, of course, depends upon how disruptive and/or dangerous the behavior might be. Obviously, some types of student behavior cannot be ignored (this suggested to Ms. Smith that the time she was using to criticize one student for inappropriate behavior might well be spent praising another for appropriate behavior).

3. Teacher behavior such as criticism should not be neglected entirely, but rather there should be a ratio between praise and criticism, with the former occurring about five times as often as the latter (it has been demonstrated that such a ratio can achieve success; moreover, it has been shown that when things are going poorly in the class-room, teachers criticize students about four or five times more than they praise them; Ms, Smith's behavior had been almost entirely one of criticism).

4. When a teacher criticizes a student, it can be done quietly. Conversely, when praise is given it can be done with emphasis. Thus, a general principle might be, *maximize the tone of praise* and *minimize the tone of criticism*. The importance of this has been

borne out in studies showing that a loud tone of criticism may likely cause more inappropriate behavior of some students while soft tones may contribute to better control situations for students. (Ms. Smith remembered that in most all cases she had resorted to shouting at students).

5. It may be a good practice for a teacher to criticize inappropriate behavior without heaping too much criticism upon a student. For example, a teacher could emphasize the fact that the student is a "good person" but that the behavior was not so good. Or, from a negative point of view "You are not a bad person, but what you did was not good behavior."

With the above information to use as a general guideline, Ms. Smith was ready to set about formulating a plan of intervention. The major objective was to make an effort to reduce or eliminate the inappropriate behavior or criticism accompanied by shouting, and replace it with a more appropriate behavior.

Ms. Smith's task was to intervene with activities that would have some influence on the above situation, and in addition, to provide for self-reinforcement of her new behavior towards the students. Following are some of the items used in the intervention plan.

1. An effort was made to use praise for appropriate behavior, not only of a verbal nature but also in the form of smiling, nods of approval, and the like.

2. An effort was made to use less criticism, based upon the undesirability of a given student behavior.

3. A new voluntary seating plan was devised for the purpose of separating those students who tended to talk out to each other.

4. Cooperative assistance of some of the students was enlisted. This took the form of notifying Ms. Smith when she tended to perform an inappropriate behavior. This action on the part of Ms. Smith indicated to her students that she was "human" after all.

The next point of concern was that of self-reinforcement. It should be recalled that self-reinforcement is concerned with overt or covert consequences in the form of statements to one's self or the acquisition of an item as a reward for one's efforts. Ms. Smith decided that the major form of self-reinforcement would involve self-praise, or what is referred to as "stroking." That is, there is a human need to be applauded for a successful effort, if not by someone else, then by one's self.

In our hypothetical model, a plan was introduced by Ms. Smith whereby when any member of the class did well in something, that person literally gave himself or herself a pat on the back. This also included Ms. Smith, and it became a common practice for her, as well as class members, to applaud themselves for a job well done. As far as overt consequences were concerned, occasionally, Ms. Smith treated herself to certain luxuries that she had previously been denying herself, such as dining out or purchasing a pair of exotic earrings. (*Note*: The reader is cautioned to remember that the above discussion is hypothetical and perhaps for the purpose of clarifying some points, aspects of it border on "theoretical extremity").

Evaluating the Plan of Intervention

The final step is concerned with how well the plan of intervention is succeeding; the extent to which the changes in behavior are achieving desired results. This process requires the development of valid evaluative criteria. These criteria can be broad in scope, and thus apply to any problems of self modification of behavior, or they can be more specific and be applied to a particular case. Some examples of general criteria might include the following:

1. In general, was there an increase in appropriate behavior and/or a decrease in inappropriate behavior?
2. What were the behaviors that achieved the most satisfactory results?
3. What forms of reinforcement appeared to be most successful?

The general evaluative criteria could be applied more specifically to our hypothetical case as follows.

1. Did Ms. Smith notice fewer instances of criticism and shouting on her part by actually keeping an account of this type of behavior? If so, how many?
2. Did the voluntary change in seating have any influence on the students who had been "talking out?" If so, in how many instances?

3. Did the system of "patting ourselves on the back" help as a reinforcer in behavior change? If so, in how many ways?

Whatever way one decides to evaluate the plan of intervention, there is still another decision to be made. This also concerns the extent to which the plan has achieved success. If it has met with complete and unequivocal success, the plan can then perhaps be terminated. Or, if it succeeds only when the behavior change is still being practiced, there may be a need to maintain the procedure. Perhaps the ultimate goal should be to modify behavior to the extent that the problem be completely eliminated. This can be accomplished if one conscientiously and systematically carries out the general procedures outlined above. Experience has shown that one can modify her own behavior not only to correct stress arousal, but to avoid it as well.

You Can Desensitize Yourself to Stress

Systematic desensitization, a form of behavior modification, can be described as the process of systematically lessening a specific learned fear in an individual. It is purported to provide a means of controlling anxiety. If one can accomplish this, it becomes extremely important in reducing stress. The reason for this is that the individual becomes more able to control her fears and anxieties. From the point of view of a clinical psychotherapeutic procedure, systematic desensitization consists of repeatedly presenting to the imagination of the deeply relaxed person the feeblest item in a list of anxiety-evoking stimuli, until no more anxiety is evoked. The next item on the list is presented, and so on, until eventually even the strongest of the anxiety-evoking stimuli fails to evoke any stir of anxiety in the person. It is the purpose of this section of the chapter to provide information for the reader that should help her understand the process of this technique and at the same time give consideration to *self*-administration for the ultimate purpose of reducing stress.

Originally, the focus of systematic desensitization was primarily upon counselor-client, therapist-patient, or teacher-student relationships, and was used as a behavior therapy technique. In recent years, systematic desensitization has gained some favor as a self-administered technique. Although the value of it as a means of lessening stress-provoking situations has not been completely established by behavioral scientists, some of the research findings are indeed encouraging. For example, studies have shown that self systematic desensitization can be very effective in overcoming severe public speaking anxiety, test anxiety, and a host of other stress-invoking stimuli.

Systematic self-desensitization efforts are not likely to be harmful, even if they fail. However, self-desensitization should be approached as an experimental procedure and should be discontinued if the course of anxiety-reduction is not relatively smooth, and should be discontinued immediately in any increase in anxiety is experienced.

Systematic desensitization can be introduced with the idea that many anxieties that people experience are due to what are termed *conditioned reactions*. These conditioned reactions are identified as stimuli that occur together in our experience and become associated with each other so that we respond to them in the same way, or in a highly similar way, when they occur again. This is to say that if we are made anxious in the presence of certain stimuli these same stimuli will make us anxious when they occur later, even if the situation no longer poses an actual threat. An example is a person who may have had a number of experiences as a child in which one in authority, such as a school principal, policeman, or guard frightened the child and perhaps punished her in some way. Such a person's reactions as an adult to one in authority may produce considerably more anxiety than the situation really justifies. This is because of the previous conditioning of strong anxiety to an authority figure.

Many of our emotions seem to be based on such conditioned reactions. These reactions are somewhat similar to reflexes, but they are learned rather than inherited (the reader is asked to refer back to the discussion of learned and unlearned tensions in Chapter 2) Their automatic "reflexive" character, however, explains why it is difficult to discuss things rationally with someone who is emotionally involved in a situation. The person is responding more with her conditioned reactions to the present stimuli than relating to the actual realities of the situation.

The recommendation for overcoming anxieties in the form of conditioned reactions is the use of systematic self-desensitization. A highly persuasive case can be made for its effectiveness, provided it is done properly.

After a particular problem has been identified, the process consists of three sequential steps: (1) developing a hierarchy of anxiety-invoking stimuli, (2) complete relaxation, and (3) desensitization sessions. Using the previously mentioned authority figure example, let us apply this to an administrative assistant who has difficulty where a relationship with her supervisor is concerned. The first step is to take several index cards, writing a different situation or experience on each card that causes anxiety. The cards are then stacked in order with the one causing the least anxiety on the top and the one causing the greatest anxiety on the bottom. This is the hierarchy of anxiety-evoking stimuli and might resemble the following.

1. Entering parking lot and seeing supervisor's car.
2. Greeting fellow employees and discussing supervisor.
3. Greeting fellow employee who mentions her coming meeting with the supervisor.
4. Conferring with a fellow employee after her meeting with the supervisor.
5. Walking by supervisor's office when door is closed.
6. Walking by supervisor's office when door is open (no verbalization or eye contact).
7. Walking by supervisor's office when door is open using eye contact and nodding.
8. Arranging meeting with supervisor's secretary.
9. Talking with supervisor's secretary about the supervisor.
10. Pre-arranged meeting with supervisor with secretary present.
11. Pre-arranged meeting with supervisor with only self present.
12. Other meetings with supervisor with only self present.

Another possible stress-inducing situation that concerns many individuals is that of making a report in front of a group. A hierarchy that could be used for self desensitization follows.

1. Reading an article about giving reports.
2. Reading report alone.
3. Reading report in front of mirror.
4. Reading report into tape recorder and playing back.
5. Reading report to a friend.
6. Reading report to a friend with another friend present.
7. Reading report with three friends present.
8. Reading report to two or three others where there is a large gathering, such as the lunch room.
9. Entering the room where report is to be given.
10. Member of audience while other reports are given.
11. Giving report to entire group.

Of course the reader must understand that the above hierarchies of anxiety-evoking stimuli are general in nature and each individual would make her own list in more detail and pertaining more to specific anxieties.

The second step is to try to develop a condition of complete relaxation (the reader is referred back to Chapter 10 for a review of the various relaxation procedures). It is recommended that the person go through each of the muscle groups in sequential order to learn to relax them one by one.

After the person is completely relaxed, the next step is the beginning of systematic self desensitization. This is done as follows. Look at the top card on the pile – the one that is the least anxiety provoking. Close the eyes, and using the imagination, visualize as vividly as possible the situation described on it. That is, one imagines the situation occurring and that she is actually there. At this point, if some anxiety is experienced, the imaginary scene should cease immediately and the person should go back to relaxing. After complete relaxation is again obtained, the person is ready to proceed. This procedure is continued until the scene can be imagined without anxiety. This may take only one or two times, or it could take 15 to 20 times, but it should be repeated until no anxiety is felt. The entire procedure is continued until one has gone through all the cards.

It is recommended that one work on the scenes in this manner for approximately one half hour at a time. It can be done daily, every other day, or a couple of times a week, depending upon the amount of time one is willing or able to spend, and how quickly one wants to conquer the anxiety. It appears to be a good practice to overlap one or two items from one session to another; that is, beginning a session by repeating an item or two from the previous session that were imagined without anxiety.

One variation of the above procedure is to tape record a description of each scene in advance. One then relaxes and listens to the tape. If anxiety appears, the recorder is turned off and the person goes back to relaxing. When relaxation is again accomplished the individual proceeds as before. A value of using the tape recorder is that there is likely to be better pronunciation, enunciation, and intonation of words. In addition, it may be easier for the individual to concentrate, since she has provided her own auditory input on tape and does not have the additional task of verbalizing and trying to concentrate on the scene at the same time. If desired, the sequence of relaxation procedures can be taped as well.

After one has been desensitized, she can review in her own mind the preferred action to take in the situation that caused anxiety. Plans can then be made to do the right thing the next time the situation occurs.

Obviously, the success one experiences with this procedure will depend largely upon the extent to which one is willing to make the painstaking effort involved in the approach. Many persons who have tried it have been so delighted by its effects that they have deliberately sought out situations that previously had caused them great anxiety, frustration and failure. This is certainly a true test of faith in the approach.

COPING BEHAVIORS THAT CAN REDUCE STRESS

Since the focus of this final chapter is on the subject of behavior, it seems appropriate to conclude with a discussion of *coping behaviors* that can reduce stress. These coping behaviors are expressed as *principles of living* that most persons can apply in helping to control stress.

In the present context the term *principle* means *guide to action*. Thus the following principles (coping behaviors) should be considered as guidelines, but not necessarily in any particular order of importance. Moreover, it should be recognized that each principle is not a separate entity onto itself. This means that all of the principles are in some way interrelated and interdependent upon each other.

Principle:
Personal health practices should be carefully observed.

Comment:
This is an easy principle to accept, but sometimes it is difficult to implement. No one is against health, but not everyone abides by those practices that can help maintain a suitable level of health. Some jobs, with their imposing schedules, may cause workers to neglect the basic requirements that are essential for the human organism to reach an adequate functional level.

Current thinking, which suggests that the individual assume more responsibility for her own health, makes it incumbent upon all of us not to pay attention to such important needs as diet, adequate sleep and rest, sufficient physical activity, and balancing work with play, all of which can reduce one's ability to cope with the stressful conditions that are inherent in our daily lives.

Principle:
There should be continuous self-evaluation.

Comment:

The practice of constantly taking stock of one's activities can help minimize problems encountered in various aspects of one's environment. This can be accomplished in part by taking a little time at the end of each day for an evaluation of the events that occurred during the day, and reactions to those events. Setting aside this time period to review performance is not only important to the achievement of goal's, but it is also important to remaining objective. Those who take time to do this will be more likely to identify certain problems over which they have no control, and thus, will try to make an adjustment until such time that a positive change can be effected. The particular time this task is performed is an individual matter; it is not recommended, though, that it be done immediately at the end of the day. A little time should be taken to "unwind" before evaluating actions that took place during the day.

Principle:

Learn to recognize your own accomplishments.

Comment:

One must learn to recognize her own accomplishments and praise herself for them, especially if such praise is not offered by others. This is generally known as "stroking" or "patting one's self on the back." (Recall the action taken by the hypothetical Ms. Smith.) In practicing this procedure one can develop positive attitudes and/or belief systems about her own accomplishments and thus reduce stress. All too often, many people "sell themselves short" and do not give themselves credit for the important things that they accomplish.

Principle:

Learn to take one thing at a time.

Comment:

This is concerned with time budgeting and procrastination. Many people are likely to put things off, and as a consequence, frustrations can build up as tasks pile up. There is a need to sort out those tasks in order of importance and attack them one at a time. Proper budgeting of time can help alleviate procrastination, which in itself can be a stress-inducing factor. Budgeting of time can help eliminate worries of time urgency and the feeling of "too much to do in too short a time."

Principle:

Learn to take things less seriously.

Comment:

This should not be interpreted to mean that important things should not be taken seriously. It does mean that there can be a fine line between what is actually serious and what is not. Sometimes when people look back at a particular event, they may wonder how they could have become so excited about it. Those persons who are able to see the humorous side in their environments tend to look at a potentially stressful situation more objectively, and this can assist in keeping stress levels low.

Principle:

Do things for others.

Comment:

People can sometimes take their mind off their own stressful conditions by offering to do something for other persons. When individuals are helpful to others, in attempting to relieve them of stress, they in turn will tend to be relieved of stress themselves. Research tends to show that those persons who volunteer to help others often get as much, or more benefit from this practice as those they volunteer to help. This even occurs in children because it has been clearly demonstrated that older children who have reading problems improve in their own reading ability when they assist younger children with these same problems.

Principle:

Talk things over with others.

Comment:

People sometimes tend to keep things to themselves, and as a consequence, they may not be aware that others may be disturbed by the same things. Sometimes discussing something with fellow workers can help one to see things in a much different light. It is important to keep in mind that such discussion should be positive and objective lest it degenerate into idle gossip. This, of course, can tend to cause deterioration of a situation that is already at a low ebb.

Principle:

Stress should not be confused with challenge.

Comment:

People often relate stress to producing tensions and therefore expect anxiety to result. Contrary to this, constructive stress in the right amounts can challenge a person and promote motivation, thinking, and task completion. Thus, recognizing stress as a natural phenomenon of life is no doubt one of the first and most important steps in dealing with it.

Coming full circle, I repeat myself by saying that the main purpose of this book is to take into account many stressful conditions that are relevant to women. Hopefully the reader has become more familiar with some of the basic facets and ramifications concerned with stress as well as possible actions women can take in dealing with it.

REFERENCES

CHAPTER 1

[1] de Beauvoir, Simone, *The Second Sex,* New York, Vintage, 1974, p. 24.

[2] Johnson, Warren R., *Human Sex and Sex Education,* Philadelphia, Lea & Febiger, 1963, p. 84.

[3] *The New Columbia Encyclopedia,* New York, Columbia University Press, 1975, p. 1974. Pell Institute for the Study of Opportunity in Higher Education, National Center for Educational Statistics, Washington, DC, 2002.

[4] Fletcher, Michael A., Degrees of Separation, Washington, DC, *The Washington Post,* June 25, 2002, p. Al.

[5] Zahniser, J.D., *And Then She Said,* St. Paul, Caillech Press, 1989, p. 37.

[6] Chisholm, Shirley, *Unbought and Unbossed,* Boston, Houghton Mifflin Company, 1970, p. 84.

[7] Mann, Judy, *Mann for all Seasons,* New York, Martin Media Ltd., 1990, p. 124.

[8] Von Drehle, David and Lydersen, Kari, Moseley-Braun Enters Democratic Presidential Race, Washington, DC, *The Washington Post,* February 19, 2003, p. A2.

[9] Goodman Ellen, Why Aren't Women Running? Washington, DC, *The Washington Post,* February 8, 1992, p. 12.

[10] The Female Electorate Washington, DC, February 17, 1992, p. 14.

[11] Fanfare, Washington, DC, *The Washington Post,* February 17. 1992, p. D2.

[12] Lawyers in Distress Reflect Displeasure with Working Conditions, Washington, DC, *Health,* March 1992, p. 3.

[13] McDowell, Jeanne, Are Women Better Cops? Time, February 17. 1992, p. 13.

[14] Warner, Rebecca L. and Steel Brent S., Affirmative Action in Times of Fiscal Stress and Changing Value Priorities: The Case of Women in Policing, *Public Personnel Management,* Fall 1989, p. 74.

[15] Vare, Ethlie, and Ptacek, Greg, *Mothers of Invention, From the Bra to the Bomb, Forgotten Women and Their Unforgettable Ideas,* Windsor, CA, National Women's History Project.

CHAPTER 2

[1] Selye, Hans, *Stress Without Distress,* New York, New American Library, 1975, p. 18.

[2] Walker, C. Eugene, *Learn to Relax; 13 Ways to Reduce Tension,* Englewood Cliffs, NJ, Prentice Hall, Inc., 1975, p. 16.

[3] Viscott, David, *The Language of Feelings,* New York, Arbor House, 1976, p. 93.

[4] Thomas, William C., Avoiding Burnout: Hardiness as a Buffer in College Athletics, Reston, VA, *Research Quarterly for Exercise and Sport,* Supplement 69, 1998 p. 116.

[5] Small, Gary, *The Memory Bible,* New York, Hyperion, 2002, p. 77.

[6] Cannon, Walter B., *The Wisdom of the Body,* New York, W.W. Norton, 1932, p. 27.

[7] Posner, Israel and Leitner, Lewis, Eustress vs. Distress: Determination by Predictability and Controllability of the Stressor, *Stress, The Official Journal of the International Institute of Stress and Its Affiliates,* Summer, 1981, Vol. 2, No. 2, p. 10.

[8] Mikhail, Anis, Stress: A Psychological Connection, *The Journal of Human Stress,* June 1981, p. 33.

[9] Small, Gary, *The Memory Bible,* New York, Hyperion, 2002, p. 64.

[10] Bremner, J. Douglas, *Does Stress Damage the Brain? Understanding Trauma-Related Disorders from Neurological Perspective,* New York, W.W. Norton, 2002, p. 12.

[11] Coburn, Christine, Is Stress Damaging Your Looks? *Health,* April 2002, p. 98.

[12] Friedman, Meyer and Rosenman, Ray H., *Type A Behavior and Your Health,* New York, Alfred A. Knopf, 1974, p. 77.

[13] Annual Meeting of the American Psychiatric Association, Dallas, May 1985.

[14] Newberry, Benjamin, A Holistic Conceptualization of Stress and Disease, No. 7 in the series, *Stress in Modern Society,* James H. Humphrey, Editor, New York, AMS Press, Inc., 1991, p. 87.

CHAPTER 3

[1] Cornwall, Patricia, *Portrait of a Killer,* New York, G.P. Putnam's Sons, 2002, p. 17.

[2] Alien, Ala, Gender Differences in Psychosocial Characterization of Adolescent Smokers, *Research Quarterly for Exercise and Sport,* March 1992, p. 17.

[3] Haden, Tony L. and Edmundson, Elizabeth W., Gender Differences for Motivations, Consequences, and Associated Behaviors of Substance Use Among College Students, *Research Quarterly for Exercise and Sport,* March 1992, p. 75.

[4] Jacobson, B.H., Adolescent Suicide Behavior in Oklahoma, *Research Quarterly for Exercise and Sport,* March 1992, p. 45.

[5] Levy, Sandra, The Aging Woman: Developmental Issues and Mental Health, *Professional Psychology,* February 1981, p. 27.

[6] McQuade, Walter and Aikman, Ann, *Stress,* New York, E.P. Dutton and Co., Inc., 1974, p. 130.

[7] Frankenhaeuser, Marianne, Women and Men Said to Differ in Their Response to Stress, *Psychiatric News,* June 18, 1975, p. 3.

[8] Humphrey, Joy and Everly George, Perceived Dimensions of Stress Responsiveness in Male and Female Students, *Health Education,* November/December 1980, p. 27.

[9] Rosch, Paul J., Are Women More Stressed Out Than Men. The News*letter of the American Institute of Stress,* No. 7, 1997, p. 5.

[10] Huget, Jennifer, A Matter of Life and Death, *KidsPost,* January 10, 2003, p. 19C.

CHAPTER 4

[1] Greenberg, Jerrold S., *Stress and Sexuality,* New York, AMS Press, Inc., 1987, James H. Humphrey Editor, p. 47.

[2] Cornwall, Patricia, *Portrait of a Killer,* New York, G.P. Putnara's Sons, 2002, p. 18.

[3] Furst, M. Laurance and Morse, Donald R. *The Woman's World*, New York, AMS Press, Inc., 1988, No. 16 in series *Stress in Modern Society*, James H. Humphrey, Editor, p. 92.

[4] Cornwell, Patricia, *Portrait of a Killer*, New York, G.P. Putnam's Sons, 2002, p. 17.

[5] Sullivan, John and Foster, Joyce Cameron, *Stress and Pregnancy*, New York, AMS Press, Inc., 1989, No. 8 in series *Stress in Modern Society*, James H. Humphrey, Editor, p. 17.

[6] Sullivan, John, Stress, Symptom Proneness and Minor Symptoms During Pregnancy, In *Human Stress: Current Selected Research*, Vol. 1, New York, AMS Press, Inc., 1986, James H. Humphrey, Editor, p. 114.

[7] Baldwin, Sharon, Sexual Harassment: Cracking Down, American College Network, *National College Newspaper*, February 1992, p. 1.

[8] Reid, T.R., Air Force Secretary Laments Scandal, Washington, DC, *The Washington Post*, February 2003, p. A2.

[9] Thakkar, R.R., and McCanne, T.R., The Effects of Daily Stressors on Physical Health of Women with and without a Childhood History of Sexual Abuse, *Child Abuse and Neglect*, February 2000, p. 209.

CHAPTER 5

[1] Whitehead, D'Ann, Use of Systematic Desensitization in the Treatment of Children's Fears, No. 1 in series *Stress in Modern Society*, New York AMS Press, Inc., James H. Humphrey, Editor, 1984, p. 213.

[2] Watson, J.B. and Raynor, R., Conditioned Emotional Reactions, *Journal of Experimental Psychology*, March 1920, p. 1.

[3] Mower, O.H., A Stimulus Response Analysis of Anxiety and Its Role as a Reinforcement Agent, *Psychological Review*, 46, 1939, p. 553.

[4] Zimmerman, Jean and Reavill, G.T., The Crying Game, *Working Mothers*, March 2002, p. 55.

CHAPTER 6

[1] Morse, Donald R. and Pollack, Robert L., The Stress-Free Anti-Aging Diet, No. 3 in the series *Stress in Modern Society*, James H. Humphrey, Editor, New York, AMS Press, Inc., 1989, p. 129.

[2] Palm, J. Daniel, *Diet Away Your Stress, Tension and Anxiety*, New York, Doubleday and Company, Inc., 1976, p. 97.

[3] Rosch, Paul J., Supplements to Reduce Stress, *The Newsletter of The American Institute of Stress,* No. 6, 1997, p. 5.

[4] Vedantam, Shanker, Study Links 8 Hour's Sleep to Shorter Life Span, Washington, DC, *The Washington Post,* February 15, 2002, p. A2.

[5] Rosch, Paul J., Sleep, Memory and Brain Functions, *The Newsletter of The American Institute of Stress,* No. 8, 1996, p. 3.

[6] WTOP Radio News Broadcast, Washington, DC, April 29, 2003.

CHAPTER 7

[1] Downey, Kirstin, Women Rising in Corporate Ranks, Washington, DC, *The Washington Post,* November 19, 2002, p. 1E.

[2] Steps to Cut Stress on the Job, *National Underwriters Property and Casualty/Risk Benefit,* Management Edition, August 1992, p. 7.

[3] Meaney, Catherine, Industrial Relations, Worksite Stress Reduction and Employee Well-being: A Participating Action Research Investigation, *Journal of Organizational Behavior,* September 1993, p. 14.

[4] Gilbert, Evelyn, Stress Common for Working Women, National *Underwriters,* September 23, 1991, p. 2.

[5] Sims, Henry and Manz, Charles, *Business Without Bosses: How Self-Managing Teams are Producing High-Performing Companies,* New York, John Wiley and Sons, 1993.

[6] Bruening, John C., Women's Stress Quotient Climbing, *Occupational Hazards,* August 1988, p. 48.

[7] Lundberg, U. Psychological and Physiological Stress Responses During Work on the Assembly Line, *Work and Stress,* March 1989, p. 47.

[8] Siegrist, J. and Klein, D., Occupational Stress and Cardiovascular Reactivity in Blue Collar Workers, *Work and Stress,* March 1990, p. 72.

[9] LaDou, J., Health Effects of Shift Work, *Western Journal of Medicine,* March 1989, p. 16.

CHAPTER 8

[1] Jacoby, Susan, The Nursing Squeeze, *AARP Bulletin,* May 2003, p. 6.

CHAPTER 9

[1] Humphrey, James H., Teenagers Will Be Teenagers, Hauppauge, NY, Nova Science Publishers, Inc., 2002, p. 10.

CHAPTER 10

[1] Benson, Herbert, *The Relaxation Response,* New York, William Morrow and Company, Inc., 1975.

[2] Jacobson, Edmund, *You Must Relax,* 4th edition, New York, McGraw-Hill, 1962.

[3] Hales, Diane and Hales, Robert, Exercising the Psyche, *Health*, June 5, 1985, p. 4.

[4] Sethi, Amarajit, Meditation as an Intervention in Stress Reactivity, in series *Stress in Modern Society,* New York, AMS Press, Inc., 1989, James H. Humphrey, Editor, p. 88.

[5] Bloomfield, Harold, *TM Discovering Inner Energy,* Boston, G.K. Hall, 1976, p. 7.

[6] Brown, Barbara B., *New Mind New Body,* New York, Bantam Books, Inc. 1975, p. 5.

CHAPTER 11

[1] Knapp, T.J. and Shodahl, S.A., Ben Franklin as a Behavior Modifier: A Note, *Behavior Therapy,* April 1974, p. 46.

INDEX